Praise for *The Decision Makeover*

"Mike Whitaker takes you through a step-by-step process to become more aware of your decisions, and the impact they will have on your life. By identifying your goals and connecting your choices to them, he helps you achieve what you want—whether in your career, relationships, or personal happiness. This handy guide should be required reading for anyone who longs for clarity and long-term success."

—LAURIE SUDBRINK, President, Unlimited Coaching Solutions, Author of *Leading with Grit*

"Both practical and inspirational, Mike Whitaker's advice reveals that each decision you make is really a fork in the road. There is no straight line to success, but the more good choices you make, the faster you will get where you want to be. It's the kind of book that you can refer to over and over again."

—ALAN C. FOX, Bestselling author of *People Tools*

"In my research and work, I have found that how people make decisions has a direct impact on outcomes. Mike Whitaker's straightforward approach helps encourage people to be more intentional about the choices they make. I highly recommend *The Decision Makeover* for anyone who wants practical advice they can apply to change their life for the better."

—JULIA TANG PETERS, Author of *Pivot Points* and Executive Coach

An Intentional Approach to

LIVING THE LIFE YOU WANT

THE DECISION MAKEOVER

MIKE WHITAKER

GREENLEAF
BOOK GROUP PRESS

Published by Greenleaf Book Group Press
Austin, Texas
www.gbgpress.com

Distributed by Greenleaf Book Group

For ordering information or special discounts for bulk purchases, please contact Greenleaf Book Group at PO Box 91869, Austin, TX 78709, 512.891.6100.

Design and composition by Greenleaf Book Group
Cover design by Greenleaf Book Group
Emoji art supplied by EmojiOne.

Cataloging-in-Publication data is available.

Print ISBN: 978-1-62634-426-6

eBook ISBN: 978-1-62634-427-3

Part of the Tree Neutral® program, which offsets the number of trees consumed in the production and printing of this book by taking proactive steps, such as planting trees in direct proportion to the number of trees used: www.treeneutral.com

TreeNeutral®

Printed in the United States of America on acid-free paper

17 18 19 20 21 22 10 9 8 7 6 5 4 3 2 1

First Edition

To Mom, Dad, Mark, and Amy.

Rock,

Chalk,

Jayhawk.

CONTENTS

FOREWORD

How many self-help books have most of us read? Plenty! Here is one that stands out from the crowd by clearly presenting the fundamentals of the component that underlies every self-help strategy—*how to make the best choices for ourselves.* Mike Whitaker has combined wisdom, wit, and proven process for sorting and selecting personal best decisions. With directness, humor, and clear illustrations, the author helps us almost effortlessly move through what can be a confusing maze of choices. A pathway is presented for first focusing readers on their lives to achieve personal success, and then becoming aware of tendencies for missteps often taken. *The Decision Makeover* guides the reader's reflection about the consequences of past actions—positive and negative—so that future actions can be guided by a rational process leading to greater personal success. By focusing thought, commitment, and action on future consequences, and kindly but unequivocally guiding the reader along a stepped decision process, it becomes clear how focus on one's Prime Goal and subordinating other decisions to accomplishing this goal is a compelling prescription for a better life.

This book is more than a litany of do's and don'ts, although one can clearly see the steps and how to carry them out. The author uses a range of examples from his successful business career, marriage, and family life to young adult decisions, focusing on the development of effective growth, facing the downside of poor decisions, and guiding the way forward through personal empowerment. These strong, very real examples give great "punch" to the narrative and lead the reader enthusiastically toward each next step. His insights are often embedded in sufficiently complex illustrations to permit the reader to use them directly or as metaphors, upon which to draw personal insights about the principles that effectively guide the making of large (prime) and supporting decisions. Interspersing quizzes, challenges, and reflective questions throughout the book helps the reader apply the principles of active learning, guiding the building and maintaining of a robust behavioral repertoire.

Our culture provides us with many opportunities to make life-altering choices that offer immediate gratification but also dead-end short-term benefits. *The Decision Makeover* is a valuable tool for sorting the good from the less helpful options for long-term success. We can immediately begin to eliminate poor habits and learn how to select better options in the immediate choice process, an important foundation for a better life. The more we practice *The Decision Makeover* process, the better decision makers we become. This is a highly readable, worthwhile book.

—William F. Weitzel Jr., PhD
Professor Emeritus
University of Oklahoma
Organizational Behavior and Change Management

INTRODUCTION

TRUTH: A majority of the difference between what you get in this life and what you wanted will be due to your decision making. A minority of that difference will be due to chance/luck.

Welcome! Regardless of our age, we can always make better decisions starting today. The fact that you have picked up this book says a lot about you. You are introspective, inquisitive, and you want the most out of your life. This will be a fun and interesting journey. You will grow your personal power across these next pages. Before we can make more decisions out in the world, we need to begin with some of the baseline concepts around decisions. Then, we will apply them to your world. Once you see the world with these thoughts in mind, you will have an advantage others will not have. Are you ready to begin?

I am a seasoned entrepreneur and business start-up coach. I have created many businesses, and I invest and advise in at least three new businesses each year. You can find me at mikewhitaker.com and my advisory business at ideagateway.com. I have a BS in psychology and an MBA. I am married with three kids: a college student, a high school senior, and a middle school student. I love to optimize businesses and people. Why a business will be successful or fail seems easy to answer compared to the same question for you and me. Why is anyone successful?

I have been thinking about this book for twenty years as I pieced together the factors that seemed to determine whether (or not) we get what we want in life—as a person. The question has fascinated me because society gets distracted by the headlines of the atypical/uncommon celebrity or entrepreneur, and it doesn't learn the underlying success formula for the masses. I scraped away the luck and factors we cannot affect, and I found out that successful people approach decisions with caution and make decisions via evaluation with a clear mind. It is more process and less randomness. It is more about taking control and less about being a victim. I found few exceptions to this good process when luck is not involved. So, I set out to describe in this book a new language of decision making and an approach to decision making that will work today and in one hundred years. I wanted to write this book because people like me and you are striving to achieve more with our lives while being happier doing it, and sometimes we are just one good tool away from making a big difference. I sincerely hope this book is a difference maker for you.

You should have a personal plan for this book. You should expect that you will think differently as you progress through the pages and exercises. You will become a critic of your past—but that is natural. What really matters is that you feel the skills developing in your mind and you put them into practice for your own good!

Who's Reading

Readers of all ages, types, and backgrounds will dive into this book. As I have been working with these concepts for several years, I have received feedback consistently from common groupings of readers. I describe them so you can know you aren't alone! This book is built for each of these reader groups.

GROUP 1: YOUNG, ALOOF, AND PREPARING

Without a lot of life experience, younger people, usually high school and college students, can learn early about the importance of early decisions and how some of the biggest decisions can result in unintended consequences—or make their dreams possible! Awareness of decisions and respecting a good decision can forever alter the life arc of a young person. Focus is the challenge with this group. If it's not an app on their phone, how can they function?

This group needs this book because life hasn't become so serious—yet. They don't know what they don't know. They are the people most able to self-direct their lives if they are more aware. This book can serve as fair warning and awakening to the power of their preparation years to make the critical decisions work out well for them.

GROUP 2: EARLY/MID-20S AND TESTING THE WATERS

This is the group in the most intense zone of decision making for the biggest decisions in life. Early marriages, children, school decisions, early career decisions, and more combine to severely impact their futures. This group senses the weight of life decisions but thinks it has forever to figure things out.

This group needs this book because preparation is over and the real race has begun. Their peers are competing with them to take the best of what is available. It's like the early stage of a race where the runners are fighting for position. The best jobs, the best mates, the best opportunities to be found early are at stake. This book will slow down the youthful dismissal of the moment's importance—creating an elegant pause at the prime moments where they will use the valuable tools found in this book.

GROUP 3: MID-CAREER AND QUESTIONING EVERYTHING

This is an intense time between thirty-three and fifty-five, as a lot of our earlier decision results are boomeranging back to us, and many of them aren't what we dreamed about. "Someday" has arrived, and we are uncomfortably accountable. We are questioning our career, our mate, our judgment, our potential . . . everything! Why? Because we have made enough bad decisions and they have affected our confidence in our ability to be satisfied going forward.

This group needs this book because life has never been this complicated. Amid the chaos we are asking ourselves better questions about why we are doing what we are doing and how that turns into what we thought we wanted. This book provides these people a framework to see their past, organize their present, and protect what they want for their future.

GROUP 4: POST-CRISIS AND IN NEED OF A BIG RESET

Regardless of our age, we encounter gut-busting life experiences where we are thrown off the horse and need a reset. We are tired of the same old difficulties, and something needs to change. Life, death, divorce, sickness, job loss, identity crisis, money troubles, etc. bring abrupt circumstances that deserve great care. This group is seeking a better way and they are listening. I have had the most feedback from people in this group because they are relieved to know they can start fresh and see a way to do better going forward. This book will help this reader take inventory and gain a clear head for the "what's next" in life.

The good news for each of the above groups is this: Improving our decision-making skills and completing the exercises in this book will change your life. People write me and tell me those exact words. And if you are the parent of an aloof/transitioning young adult, ***you can lead that horse to water and make them think.***

Parents: Your Teenager/Young Adult Can Use This Book

In a matter of a few years, we expect our kids to transition from student to CEO of their lives. A CEO makes a lot of decisions! What training does your child have today toward being a good CEO of their future? It defies logic to suggest that kids quickly transition from the helicopter parent making decisions for them to becoming a competent CEO of their life. Our children need coaching.

As I tested this book with readers who had teenagers and young adults, many of those parents voiced two types of thoughts:

"My child needs to read this so they don't screw up."

This is the voice of the proactive parent who wants their child to be more aware of potential pitfalls as well as maximize their potential. Simply recognizing the basic concepts in this book will give any child an advantage over others in their peer group.

"My child needs to read this because he/she is already screwing up."

This is the voice of the reactive parent who is already unhappy with the choices their child has made. The child is currently failing their parents' expectations. Portions of this book can be good conversation topics between parents and children. Rather than finger-pointing and judging, this book supports a consistent goal: getting you the life you want, regardless of when you begin a fresh start. Parents can use that stance to share concepts with their child that are good for us all.

Note to Gen Next and Millennials and Their Parents . . .

Gen-X (born in the '60s and '70s) and Gen-Y (born in the '80s and '90s) parents have tended to be "helicopter parents." In other words, we have been hovering over you, overly involved in your decision making and discovering the world for yourself. Allowing you to "skin your knee" or "learn the hard way" is hard for a helicopter parent. While this has benefited you greatly in some ways, our eagerness to succeed (via you, our children) has created a problem.

If you are a child of the 2000s and 2010s, you are maturing slower. Thirty-five percent of you are living with your parents after high school. Your parents make incredible efforts to make sure you do not fail. You have a safety net larger than any generation in history. These facts affect your long-term planning. In fact, your generation is postponing significant life decisions. You are flexible. You are likely smarter than the antiquated educational systems you've endured. You are more likely to "figure it out as you go along" in an instantaneous society wired for short-term thinking. Your generation is nicer, works together better, and is less greedy. But something important is missing: You don't know how to independently plan for success and make decisions to get you there.

We parents owe you the messages in this book: Real-world decisions that make or break your dreams and goals are coming toward you faster than is comfortable for you and/or your parents. Due to technology and global advancement, our American society is heading toward fifty percent unemployment by the year 2050. Only the strongest and best thinkers will thrive to be able to have the American Dream. We need to sit down and get prepared. Good results don't just happen to us. We are both the Uber driver and the passenger in our lives. It is your job to know where you are going and how to get there.

Let's do this.

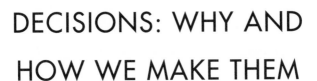

·1·

DECISIONS: WHY AND HOW WE MAKE THEM

Ouch. Have you ever had a broken heart? Lost a job? Missed an opportunity? Wished you had done the opposite of what you did? Do you carry any regrets about decisions you've made so far at this point in your life? Of course, we all can scream YES! to these questions. We have had more than one decision go bad. Sometimes, life can make us feel lucky or unlucky because the results seem to jump right into our lap—and we have to deal with them. Do you realize where these results come from?

Why does success seem more like something that happens *to us* instead of something we *create*? Most people fail to recognize the fact that ***opportunities come to us every day in the form of decisions.*** These decision opportunities can significantly change how our lives turn out, yet most people do not prepare for how they will assess a decision to yield a good outcome. In *The Decision Makeover*, you are the focus. Isn't your future worth a little focus? Of course it is!

Today, you could be in the middle of a big decision or wanting to be prepared for the next—and you may have uncertainty. How do you tend to make big decisions? Do you have a good process? How do we handle ourselves when someone or something is presented in front of us? There is much at stake and we need to think this through in a confident manner. We can prepare for the decisions that are certain to come and be ready when the opportunity arises. The results will be our own and will be the best they can possibly be.

How can anyone reach a destination without deciding to go there? How can an athlete win a race without deciding to run it? How does a lottery winner win without deciding to buy a ticket? How can a romance begin without someone deciding to break the ice? We humans are constantly making decisions, every minute of our conscious lives. In fact, what we "get out of life" is mostly dependent upon our decisions along the way. Our hearts beat and our lungs fill with air without requiring decision making. But beyond those innate functions, everything else in our lives stems from a decision we make or a decision made for us by someone else. Beyond what we decided to have for breakfast, the decisions get bigger and have more impact upon our lives. To our great credit or regret, we decide things like these: what school to attend (or not), who to marry (or not), what business to start (or not), what career/job to pursue (or not), how many children to have (or not), where to live, what makes us happy, what we will do for money, and thousands of other decisions that add up to significantly impact our lives.

Why Decisions Matter

We humans tend to make bad decisions—often. Like a cup full of holes, our bad decisions add up in our lives and drain away our forward progress toward what we really want. Think how much less effort would be required if we didn't punch so many holes into our future by making poor decisions!

Here is the bigger, better question: How do *you* make decisions? Do you make big decisions the same way you make small ones? Do you have a specific process? Do you pause to consider the consequences, or are you usually in a hurry? Most people make decisions with little thought to the long-term consequences. Bad decisions cause us pain and waste precious time in our lives. Bad decisions create regret we carry our whole lives.

However, what if there were a way to recognize the power of decisions and custom-fit those decisions to fit the life you want? What if there were a way to use every decision—both good and bad—as momentum toward a future you desire for yourself? What if you could change some bad decisions into good ones? What if you had a much greater sense of control over your life and you used good decision making to achieve it? All these things are possible as you begin your Decision Makeover, starting today. We have more power than we think. We will learn to use that power.

The Most Important Decision of Your Life

First of all, why are decisions so darn important? Think about driving and "who cares if I turn left or right?" The answer? Nobody cares until you have pinpointed a destination. Suddenly, with a destination in mind, the left turn takes you away from your destination and the right turn takes you toward it. So, ***for decisions to matter, we have to have a goal in mind.***

> *"I always have to think about what's important in life to me are these three things. Where you started, where you are, and where you're going to be."*
>
> —JIM VALVANO, IN HIS "NEVER GIVE UP" SPEECH

People often express a desire, "I want to be successful in life." I suggest that personal success is a nice goal to keep in mind. It is inspirational, it changes over time, and it should be your own definition of success. If I ask people in my network this question: "At the end of your life, when you look back over your years, if you were to describe your life as a success, how would you define that success, for you?" Their answers may surprise you:

> *"I used to think success was the quantity of the journey—the number of experiences that could be crammed in—but I now realize that success is the quality of the journey."*

> *"If my life honors my God, leaves a net positive impact on the world, and creates a foundation for my spouse and children to pursue their own success, it will have been a success."*

"If I did my very best in my various roles I played, such as the roles of son, father, provider, lover, teacher, student, companion, leader/follower, etc. within a movement or group or community."

"Success is not a static endpoint in my life. The elusiveness of it is what drives me each day to be better than I was the day before. So, it is my hope, at the true endpoint, that I can say service to God, family, and everyone else I encountered focused my drive for excellence."

"I made a difference. I was an honest person. I achieved love and happiness."

"Past successes seem to dwindle in their importance as time passes by; therefore, for me, success is a future pursuit. As I look back over my life, I am looking forward to being a person of dignity wrapped in courtesy, endurance coupled with patience, being able to bear disappointment or sorrow without deflecting another, willing and able to share wisely whatever knowledge I may possess."

Thus, my belief: Better decision making allows people to be in the position to achieve success—however people wish to define it for themselves.

Let's take a moment and visualize the thoughtful moment in the future when you are evaluating your life. There will be one decision, as you look back, that you will easily label as the most important decision you ever made, whether it turned out well or poorly. However, there will be a dozen decisions that you will consider significant to the path your life has taken. What were they? Do you want to be in control of that story? The truth is that you absolutely can! The movie director knows how the story is supposed to turn out before filming the movie. You are that director for your life. Roll film! With all the opportunities and roadblocks that life throws at us, we can learn to make the best choices, with the most confidence. This makes us feel extremely good while making significant improvements to our success story. This is your opportunity. Isn't it exciting that we will change between the beginning and the end of this book?

Why We Make Decisions

We make decisions because we have to. Life requires making choices. The more roads we travel, the more possible turns we must consider. It's easy for most people. For some folks, big decisions are anxiety-ridden burdens. But everyone has to answer yes or no, choose left or right, decide to leave or stay, choose him or her, select vanilla or chocolate, etc. The number of decisions we make is so large we don't even notice how often we are deciding something. ***Decisions are break points in our journey, regardless of how trivial, that determine the next moment or the next twenty years.*** Once we decide, the alternative choices can no longer be chosen and are lost for now, or forever. Not making a decision, choosing none of the options, is difficult because we desire to make progress toward what we want. Life brings decisions because we have needs and other people demand action from us. Each decision is a step in life. Our decisions are steps forward, sideways, or backward.

How We Usually Make Decisions

Ask someone, "How do you make decisions?" and watch their facial expression. It's an odd question, but it shouldn't be odd. It's something we humans do every five minutes of every waking hour. Their answer should be nearly as easy as responding to, "How do you get out of bed in the morning?" Yet the answers to our decision question are not polished. Some people shrug their shoulders and say, "I dunno. I just think about it for a moment." Others say, "I do what feels right to me." If we inject honesty into most answers, "How do you make decisions?" would be answered this way: "I make decisions by trial and error . . . and I try not to repeat the error." In driving, when I make a wrong turn, I resolve to only do it once. Next time I will remember and avoid the problem. So trial and error works, right? Wrong.

Here's why trial and error, the most commonly used decision-making strategy, absolutely fails to deliver life success for people: Trial and error fails because we select at least one of our options each time—when the best choice for us may be to choose *none*. Perhaps none of the choices fits what is best for our success.

Trial and error fails because what we remember is only why the error was bad. Do we get where we want by taking all the wrong turns until, once we have eliminated them all, we have narrowed down the only right choice? I know adults who take that approach in finding a spouse, and the result is chaos. Trial and error does not focus upon why each of our options makes sense in the big picture. The question should be: *Does this choice best support my personal definition of success?*

So now that we are warming up on this decision topic, we are going to have you test your decision-making ability by looking at your experiences up to today.

Being Aware of the Real Decision

As I drive to work along my normal route, I enjoy my coffee, listen to music, and make the usual turns to reach my office and park my car. I drive this route without making a single decision. Yet, the first time I drove this route, my trip was full of decisions! Which route? Turn here? Left lane? Merge now? The mental state is important for detecting that we are approaching a decision. It would be nice if flashing red lights and crossing barriers would lower in front of us (like the train crossing on my route) when a decision is before us. Often, we are presented with a small question and, without realizing it, we are in the middle of a bigger decision. Thus, an awareness of decisions in front of us (the real decision) is essential. If we are not aware, we cannot respond appropriately.

Example 1: A coworker asks you to go out to lunch.
The decision is "Lunch? Yes or No?"

However, the bigger decision looms via a barrage of questions: "Is this a date?" "What's his situation?" "LOL, what's my situation?" "Will this affect our working relationship?" "Do I find him attractive?" "What do I wear?" etc. etc.

The bigger decision is "Am I openly dating? Yes or No?" If Yes, "Is he worthy of my time and attention? Yes or No?"

Example 2: A friend invites you to a networking event. The decision is "Do you want to attend? Yes or No?"

Often we are tired of wasting time with the wrong people. The most important factor is why you would go to this networking event. What is the bigger goal this event supports?

The bigger decision is, "Can the people attending this event directly impact my career?" Also, we can ask ourselves, "Is there a higher quality event I can attend instead of this one?"

Example 3: A realtor invites you to look at a home way above your price range. The decision is, "What time works for you to view the house on Saturday? Two p.m. or four p.m.?"

Ding, ding, ding . . . warning bells . . . This isn't a harmless activity. Once you see the house you cannot afford, the house you can afford will never be good enough. Or, you will dumbly overbuy and be stressed financially, and that leads to all kinds of damage.

The bigger question is, "Does this house qualify as a good fit?"

Example 4: A teenager is offered a cigarette. The decision is, "Do I smoke it? Yes or No?"

No teenager wants to consider at this point that they may become addicted and will spend $40,000 on cigarettes and die (on average) twenty years early.

The bigger decision is, "Am I a smoker? Yes or No?" If not, a nonsmoker doesn't smoke.

Example 5: A student visits the premium coffee shop for his daily coffee fix. Drip coffee is $2 and the latte is $5. He alternates between both choices. The decision today is: "$2 or $5?"

Since money is tight for most students, the bigger question is, "Is this the best way to spend $2,500 over four years, or should this money be allocated toward other priorities?"

Being aware of a decision and its *total* impact over time is a skill. It is like trying to train your mind to play "Where's Waldo?" and the goal is simply to find the decision and stomp your feet for recognition.

Who's Keeping Score?

Show me the kid in the game that announces "I don't want to keep score anymore" and I'll show you who is losing.

Everyone is keeping score. Regardless of your definition of success, the truth is it's a dog-eat-dog world out there: fifty applicants for every open job, limited college openings, limited income, limited investors for new businesses, limited loans from limited banks, limited quality single men and women, etc. The world is competitive! To be human is to compete. Everyone wants to win. Some are trying harder than others. Some get lucky. But there must be more losers than winners. Those are the odds. You win when you beat the odds. ***Winners have the best skills in decision making.***

Aside from defining success for a lifetime, here's another big question: What do you want out of life? The younger you are, the more difficult it is to answer that question. It's good to be selfish when asking yourself, "Yeah, what *do* I want? What is important to me?"

Do you realize that you are the *only* person on the planet thinking of those answers on behalf of *you*? That's it! Just you. So, isn't it important to be keeping some kind of score for yourself?

What I achieved
– What I wanted
My Score

Does this simple subtraction exercise create pause for you? This is a tough concept. Take heart; we dream and we plan and we watch other people—and those visions create the picture of what we want. We are good dreamers and not very good accountants when we are scoring our progress. We get a negative score when our dreams are greater than our achievements—which is painful to admit later in life. Thus, the simplest way to make this subtraction problem look better is to *lower* your expectations. That is not what you should do, but it is what people must do when they make bad decisions.

For the sake of this book's ability to help you, let's generally define life success as an ability to say to ourselves:

> *"I led a fulfilling life that challenged me in the ways I wanted to be challenged. From where I started in life, I accomplished what I wanted to accomplish. I saw the things I wanted to see, I am OK with what I did not experience. I helped people I wanted to help. I am generally pleased with the choices I made in this life."*
>
> —YOUR NAME

Would you be satisfied if you could say the above to yourself?

Undo: If Only It Were This Easy

Undo, redo, it's something I wish I could use all the time. I went left, figured out I should have gone right, and a simple "undo" would save me a whole lot of time and frustration. It's the science fiction in movies where we fantasize about being able to go back in time, even for a few seconds, and choose differently. The ultimate time machine can provide the ability to right a wrong or take the unchosen path, using hindsight to improve an outcome. However, in real life, we don't get the undo. Once someone is hurt, they're hurt. Once we say "I do," we're in. When we choose A, we have denied B through Z. When there is no undo, we're left only with, "I'm sorry." We can apologize to others and ourselves for bad decisions, but we never get the time or resources back. ***When we lose time, we lose the ability to achieve what we want in this life.***

Forks in Our Road

"If you come to a fork in the road, take it."

—YOGI BERRA

A fork is a choice you find in the path before you. Most people look at each fork as an independent event where they either choose left or right. I do not believe the forks that lead to success are independent in our lives. Rather, I believe success momentum comes from interdependent decisions that turn out to be the correct choices. It's about making a series of great decisions. A good decision opens up the next possible good decision, etc.

Remember the Plinko game on *The Price Is Right* game show? This game featured winning or losing based upon your token falling randomly and going left/right after colliding with each peg (decision) on its way down. Most people spend their lives dropping their token and hoping to land in the right place. Or, they go through life as the Plinko token and bounce as they hit each peg and try to steer left or right, yet are not in any control whatsoever. We can do so much better!

The Forks Add Up

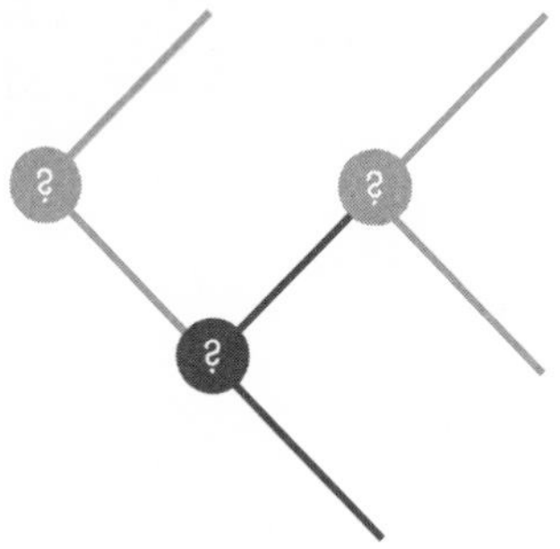

So, when we consider our decisions in life, they come one after the other. We can count, for me, for you, for anyone, the dozens of unique decisions in life that move us toward success or toward failure—depending upon our goals and choices. Each choice affects the next series of possible forks. If we drift too far from the success path, we can never reach success (see diagram). In fact, we can make the conclusion that the earlier decisions are more monumental in determining the final success outcome. Start off wrong, and you have a long road ahead with mediocre results at best. Start off right, and even if you screw up in the later forks, you can still obtain success!

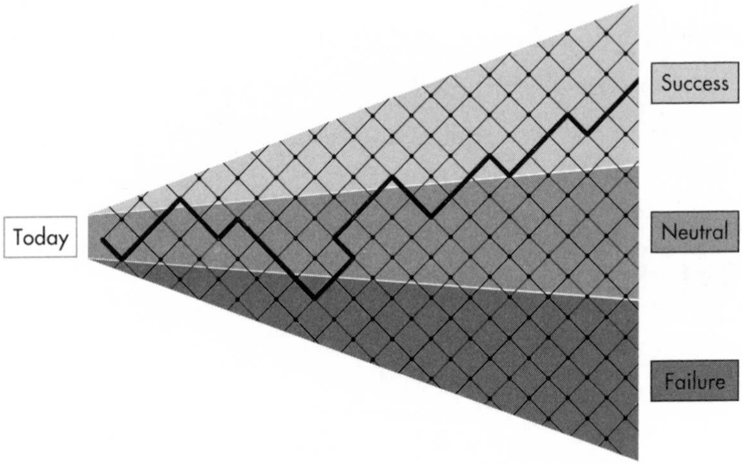

Forks Are Unavoidable

Someone who refuses to choose gets little accomplished. Try driving a car and refusing to make any turns. It is not very productive. Forks (decisions) come our way every few minutes. Using the driving example, the faster we drive, the faster the forks come at us. Hurry up, decide! We could say that your driving speed represents your *pace* toward getting to where you want to go, while your *distance* to destination represents your goals in life—the bigger the goal, the more distance required. Thus, higher expectations require more speed to cover more distance—and many more decisions made correctly. Please read that again. Good decision making allows you to pick up speed and make faster progress.

The greatest torment I have experienced in my life has been self-inflicted. I would badger myself about bad decisions. "You're so stupid!" I would lament. Well, maybe I was not stupid, but I certainly had a flaw in my approach. I began to visualize that I was forty good decisions away from success in every part of my life. Forty forks away! And then, I needed to know how to best make a decision at each fork.

PERSONAL EXERCISE:
Am I a Good or Bad Decision Maker?

Self-Assessment:

Part of understanding the power of decision making and the significant impact it makes in our lives is testing these concepts for yourself. It may be helpful if you see how well you have been able to make decisions at this point in your life. For this important exercise, please make a handwritten response. Perhaps use a separate sheet of paper to record your thoughts.

Continued

Let's break down our lives into a few key categories. How would you rate your historic decision making for the following "Biggie" questions?

1. Money: When I've had money, could I have managed it better in a way that would be helping me right now? (Yes / No)
2. Romantic Relationships: Have I spent significant time/effort in an unhealthy relationship, or did I choose the wrong person and reject the right person somewhere along the way? (Yes / No)
3. Education: Should I have gone further in my education with more advanced certifications or a different focus? (Yes / No)
4. Career: Is the work I am doing today not what I envisioned for myself and more a way to make a living? (Yes / No)
5. Opportunities: Has someone told me "take a chance" toward an opportunity that challenged me and was exhilarating—and I declined to do so but today wish I had? (Yes / No)
6. Health: If I look at my health history as well as look in the mirror right now, have I taken risks and/or led a lifestyle that has surely affected my life span and quality of life? (Yes / No)
7. Purchases: Have I purchased something that felt good at the time, but in hindsight, that purchase set me back financially and/or made it impossible to purchase something more meaningful to me? (Yes / No)
8. Friendships: Have I invested significant time/effort in a friendship that turned out to be a bad situation? (Yes / No)
9. Legal: Have I made a decision that resulted in legal trouble for me or my family or my company? (Yes / No)

10. Family: Have I made past decisions about significant family members (parents, siblings, children) that negatively affected their world? (Yes / No)
11. Future Setup: Have I made past decisions that today make me feel that I am not set up for the future I desire? (Yes / No)

Assessment Results:

By counting the number of "Yes" responses to the eleven questions above, we can roughly assess our decision-making record. The older we are, the more likely we can say yes to more questions (i.e., learning the hard way).

This quiz should help us see that we can also avoid bad decisions in these same categories by being mindful of this book's concepts! The goal is not perfection; the goal is improvement to prevent any more "Yes" answers going forward.

"YES" COUNT RATING:

1 or less: You are either a brilliant decision maker or you haven't ventured outside your home to challenge the world. You are least encumbered with decision baggage and should be able to set lifetime goals and achieve them. You can set bigger goals at this point and/or just move faster.

2 or 3: You have been a good decision maker in one area, but you have a weakness in another area of decision making. For example, we tend to be either good or poor in our people decisions, or good or poor with money, affecting several key decision categories. You are likely able to attain your objectives, but you have been delayed/hindered possibly for years by some of your decisions. Going forward, every decision counts if you want your personal vision to come true.

4 or 5: You are at moderate risk of settling for a life you didn't necessarily plan—depending upon your age. You are significantly impacted by decision baggage, and some good decisions are needed to free you from the current baggage. At this point, you must slow down and respect the power of a decision made well. Review your top goals and plot an updated course with a new discipline.

6 or 7: You are at high risk of being forced to accept a life you didn't want and may feel a little helpless to change your odds. You likely navigate loosely through life and/or you listen to too many other people—and you have steered wrongly. You can reset your situation, but you must take accurate stock of your circumstances, how you got here, who you listened to, and what you must avoid from this point forward. Every day counts for you and your decisions.

8+: You are a chronic poor decision maker. It's not like you tried to fail, but it just turned out that way. "Stop the bleeding"—as they say. You are in a constant state of problem solving, and you likely have already accepted internally that you will never achieve your life goals—if you know what they are. You need to set one goal that you can affect, and claw your way back into driving your life forward by making one good decision at a time. Every hour counts for you and your decisions.

PERSONAL EXERCISE:
Your Plan for This Book

How We Use This Book

For the rest of this book, we are going to accomplish the following:

UNDERSTANDING:

- The power of decisions
- Why we make bad decisions
- How to deal with bad decisions
- How to deal with regret
- How to take control of decision making
- Goals and decisions can help each other

CREATING ACTION PLANS:

- Adjustments we must make to fix our past and present
- Defining and prioritizing what we really want
- How to achieve the life we want with good decision making

ENJOY FEELING MORE IN CONTROL:

- Watch yourself master decisions and enjoy the rewards

·2·

THE COST OF CHOOSING POORLY

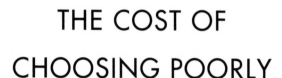

Wrong turns happen. We all make bad choices. Hopefully, we are learning on the small ones! The big mistakes have greater costs. The losses of time, energy, money, health, and opportunity are permanent. We cannot get them back. We may have learned a lesson, but it costs us in many ways to choose poorly on a big decision. Perhaps the greatest cost is what we could have done instead (the other options we had). How can we quantify what our life would have been like if we had not continued looking elsewhere and stayed with the first girl/guy we loved? That person has moved on and we will never know. How can we know if more education would have vaulted us higher? What would have happened if we had said "Yes" to that crazy idea and moved far from home? How can we know how far we could have taken our art, our sport, our dream when we made decisions away from it, postponing it? The pain of the results is compounded by the effects of second-guessing, of doubting our choices. ***We need to eliminate all types of decision pain.*** With confidence in how we make these decisions, we can better navigate the forks, handling them with excitement and anticipation and moving forward in our life plan.

Bad Decision Effects

Let's look at the effects and how long they last—when we make bad decisions:

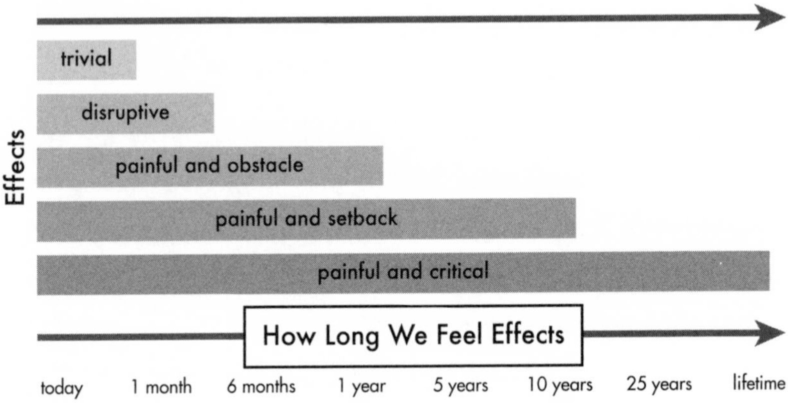

Effect—Trivial: Hopefully, this is where we do the most experimenting. These effects come from decisions we make that reveal their impact in the short term. Costs are low. Chances of regret are low. Pain of regret is low. Decisions include what clothes we wore today, where we had lunch, what TV shows we watched, what we surfed on the web, what we texted on our phone, etc. Our days are full of these types of decisions. No single instance will harm us if we choose poorly. However, it may reflect how many friends you have!

Effect—Disruptive: A decision that creates a disruptive result has knocked us off our game, requiring us to adjust our approach, our timeline, our budget, etc. The key to this impact type is: Adjustment is possible at a low cost. Pain and regret are minimized because we can fix it; a short amount of time is lost. Decisions include the early phases of the dating game with a specific person, slightly offending someone we care about, missing work, forgetting an appointment, spending too much for dinner or while shopping, failing to stay in touch with someone who is important to us (personally or career-wise), etc. Decision failures in this category absorb extra time and effort that we could have spent elsewhere (similar to tapping on the brakes while driving).

Effect—Painful and Obstacle: Thomas A. Edison said the following about obstacles encountered via invention: "I have not failed. I've just found ten thousand ways that won't work." Every time we find a way that won't work, we have learned something hopefully valuable in the overall pursuit that will continue. However, it slows us down when we reach an obstacle, turn around, and adjust for what we have learned. We cannot tolerate too many failures in this category because they cost us a year of our lives and/or momentum. Costs can be high. Chances of regret are low. Pain of regret is low. Decisions include taking a new job to see if we like it or to learn (internship), dating exclusively, taking a class, extended travel to new places (exploring), starting a new hobby, doing nothing for a while, paying attention (or not) to someone important to us (personal or career-wise), saving money (for a rainy day), etc.

Effect—Painful and Setback: Costing us three to ten years of our lives, we hopefully keep these decisions to a minimum. A failure in this category is a setback requiring a restart, as in starting over. Decisions include choosing a college major/trade degree, multi-year exclusive dating/marital engagement, moving to a new town, starting a business, making an investment (of significant time or money), adopting a pet, etc. Costs are high. Chances of regret are high. Pain of regret is medium if we can figure out how to recover quickly.

Effect—Painful and Critical: A negative decision impact of this severity has changed us for a lifetime. We cannot escape the effects when we get it wrong. Decisions include falling in love, getting married, deciding whom to marry, buying a house, having children, deciding when to have children, making a career commitment that includes certification, sticking with and trying to grow a business, making a major financial investment, making personal health choices, etc. ***Costs are immeasurable. Regret is certain. Pain of regret is high.*** The pain is still there even if we do it right the second time, if that is even an option.

Good Questions for Questionable Decisions

When we suspect pain from a bad decision, it is helpful if we can dig further and possibly prevent lifetime catastrophe. Ask yourself some key questions about each area of bad decision effects:

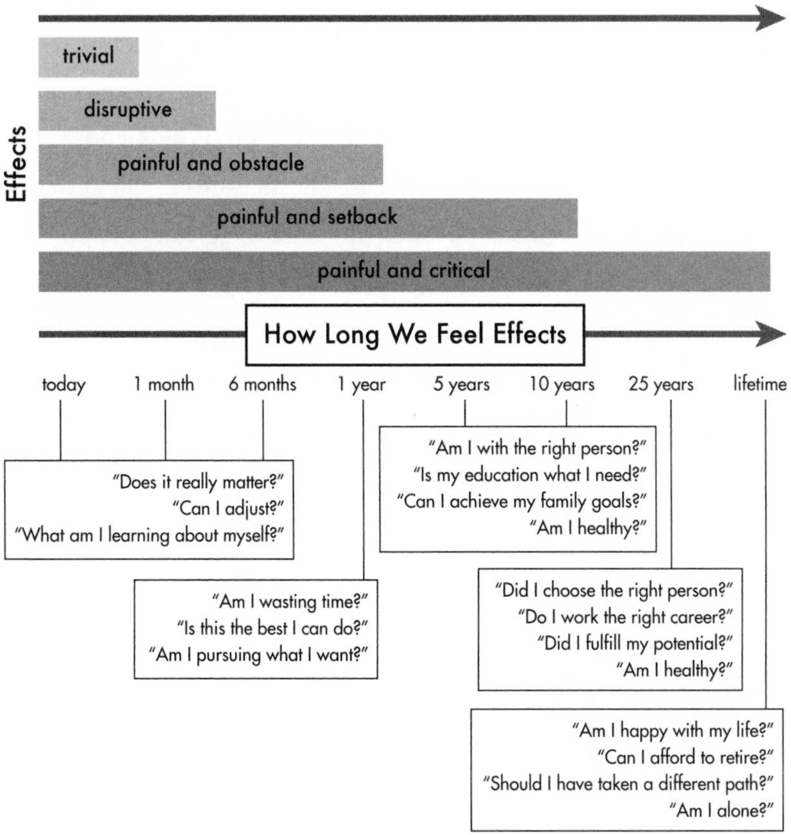

These questions are good checks and balances for you to consider if your instincts (or friends) are bugging you about a lingering bad decision. Bad decisions are weaknesses that will show up when you can least tolerate them. Bad decisions and their associated pain are like a sore tooth: It sometimes doesn't hurt until you want to use it—and then it's too late. My grandfather used to work on his farm machinery when he didn't really need to work on it. As I was standing next to him (helping), shivering or otherwise uncomfortable,

I would ask, "Why do we have to do this *today*?" There was fishing to do, in my mind. His reply was: "We do this now so the equipment is ready when we need it. We don't want it breaking down in the field." We have weaknesses due to bad decisions in our current relationships, careers, health, and many other Biggie categories. We don't want weaknesses piling up and riding along in the major areas of our life—breaking us down at the wrong times. Thus, at the first sign of bad-decision effects, investigate further to see how long you will be dealing with them.

·3·

THE SIZE OF DECISIONS

If you walk yourself through a single day, look at all the decisions you make along the way. What do you wear? What do you eat? To whom do you talk? What route do you walk or drive? How do you spend your time—work or pleasure? Do you set any new goals? Do you agree to something? Do you make any decisions—small, medium, or big?

Number of Decisions Per Year

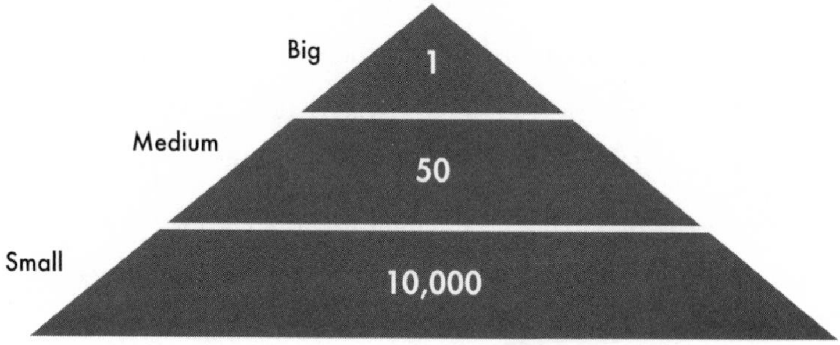

Keeping it simple, we can place decisions in three categories: small, medium, and big. If you take inventory of the decisions you have made this week, you likely made mostly small decisions and only one medium decision. So, what's a medium decision? Medium decisions are best illustrated as "course corrections"—like a boat captain. Since the boat's destination is one of our big decisions, then along the way, we have to make small turns, speed up, slow down, refuel, etc. These medium decisions assure progress toward our success. For example, if a big decision is "get this college degree," then a medium decision would be to take a course that advances us in that degree, and a small decision would be to study tonight. What makes anyone a good boat captain? Answer: an awareness of the destination, our current position, heading, speed, *and* the ability to swiftly make adjustments. For your life, how skilled a captain are you?

The Biggest Decisions (The Biggies)

The following decision categories are absolutely the biggest areas of decision making that make or break your future happiness and successful achievement. It is remarkable that so many people jump into them so lightly. Also, I know these are the big ones because they always make the list of people's top regrets in life. So, being aware and prepared for the Biggies is a significant advantage.

Decision Category: Education

EDUCATION AMOUNT

This decision pretty much sets your baseline income potential for your whole career (and retirement savings). For example, over a thirty-year career, total earning potential (Source: US Census 2009):

	Not a high school graduate	High school graduate only	Some college, no degree	Associate's	Bachelor's	Master's	Doctorate	Professional
Per year	20,241	30,627	32,295	39,771	56,665	73,738	103,054	127,803
Thirty-year career	607,230	918,810	968,850	1,193,130	1,699,950	2,212,140	3,091,620	3,834,090

Money isn't everything, but it is helpful fuel for what you want to do in life. The early decision in this category is super-critical. It is the difference between you being in control vs. being dependent upon others. For me, not feeling in control is one of my worst states of mind, and I will do whatever it takes to regain control. I feel the role of money for me is to assure freedom to do what I want to do instead of just what I have to do. So, when we make decisions about the amount of education we will absorb, we are setting our likely income parameters.

EDUCATION EFFORT

Parents know that cumulative effort turns into the final result, and that is why we are always imploring our kids to study. If only the kids knew what we knew: that the entire world is being separated between those who make more effort and those who do not. In 2012, the three-yearly OECD Programme for International Student Assessment (PISA) report, which compares the knowledge and skills of fifteen-year-olds in seventy countries around the world, ranked the United States fourteenth out of thirty-four OECD countries for reading skills, seventeenth for science, and a below-average twenty-fifth for mathematics. How is that possible? Effort. Subpar effort is a daily decision that we US citizens are often making, contrary to our best long-term interests.

EDUCATION GRADES/STANDARDIZED SCORES

Higher education selects its most desirable students for scholarships and admission based upon grades and standardized scores. We can no longer get into a great school based upon a fantastic personality. The grades and scores (ACT, SAT, GRE, LSAT, etc.) have to be notable.

EDUCATION SCHOOLS

Where we go to school will absolutely affect our lives. Schools have reputations. Companies, when hiring, have a bias toward and against certain schools. Attending Rural State University Tech is better than nothing, but you will lose in comparison to two hundred other college pedigrees. Counselors will tell you to go to the best school you can enter and afford. They will also tell you to consider your personal traits and how well the school fits you. That combination is a big decision.

EDUCATION DEGREES AND SPECIALTIES

What we choose for focus in education usually points to our lifetime career focus, especially if we are pursuing advanced degrees (e.g. education, medicine, law, finance, etc.). Focusing upon how we will apply ourselves to the world often consumes additional years of our life, as well as considerable expense—so we cannot choose more than one. No pressure! What we do for work will determine our income and our satisfaction. It's a huge decision.

Decision Category: Whom to Take as Life Partner and When

Does your love interest make you more productive? *Inc.* magazine reported in 2015: "Researchers at Washington University in St. Louis found that people with relatively prudent and reliable partners tend to perform better at work, earning more promotions, making more money, and feeling more satisfied with their jobs."[1]

That's true for men and women: "Partner conscientiousness" predicted future job satisfaction, income, and likelihood of promotion (even after factoring in the participants' level of conscientiousness).

> According to the researchers, "conscientious" partners perform more household tasks, exhibit more pragmatic behaviors that their spouses are likely to emulate, and promote a more

....

1 "Marrying the Right Person Makes You More Successful, According to Science" by Jeff Haden, *Inc. Magazine*, May 12, 2016. www.inc.com/jeff-haden/marrying-the-right-person-makes-you-more-successful-backed-by-science.html

satisfying home life, all of which enables their spouse to focus more on work.

So who will you choose as a life partner, if anyone? Their qualities will determine your success. Their age can be significant also. Partnerships of the same age usually last the longest.

Also critical is at what age we choose our life partner. ***People who commit to each other later in life and who dated longer have the most stable partnerships.*** Stability is important because a good partnership can demonstrate that 1+1=3.

What about love, you ask? This often surprises people: Your partner's qualities and at what age you take on a partner will make love more likely to last (and grow) between the two of you—not the other way around. Your love is not going to change your partner or the circumstances. Love rarely holds bad decisions together for long. Looking at it another way, falling in love is not a decision that can claim any accomplishment. Falling in love is usually not a goal by itself. What is *accomplished* by the partnership receives the focus thereafter. Thus, falling in love creates the temporary opportunity to form a strong partnership. However, if the partners, partnership, and/or their circumstances are flawed from the beginning, love cracks due to the strain of a poor foundation.

Decision Category: Having Children and When

Children are amazing . . . and amazingly expensive and time consuming. I have three children and would not trade the experience for anything. However, if I had had children early in life, I am certain many of my goals would have been abandoned, and I am certain I would have more anxiety over my financial future. *When* we have children matters. It is a sequence of "fit" in our individual journeys. "When does parenthood make the most sense?" That is a matter of prioritizing our goals.

The average cost of raising a child born in 2013 up until age eighteen for a middle-income family in the US is approximately $245,340 (or $304,480, adjusted for projected inflation), according to the latest annual "Cost of Raising A Child" report from the US Department of Agriculture (Aug 18, 2014).

US CENSUS DATA FROM 2000 SHOWS:

- Women who waited to have kids had significantly higher salaries than women of the same age, with the same level of education, who had kids earlier.
- For women between ages forty and forty-five with professional degrees and full-time jobs, those who gave birth to their first child at age thirty-five made more than $50,000 more per year than women who had their first child at twenty, on average. Even waiting to start a family just five more years, at thirty-five instead of thirty, made a difference of $16,000 per year, on average.
- For men, it's the opposite story (sorry, ladies). On average, men's earnings increased more than six percent when they had children (if they lived with them), while women's

> decreased four percent for each child they had. "Employers read fathers as more stable and committed to their work; they have a family to provide for, so they're less likely to be flaky." Employers rate fathers as the most desirable employees, followed by childless women, childless men, and finally mothers. The one exception is for mothers in the top 10% of jobs, who had the same income bias opportunity as men since employers consider them high performers who can negotiate.[2]

Men and women, when it comes time to make this big decision, the concepts in this book will help you define what is important to you and how to decide. Generally, the more established your career and your marriage, the more you are in a position to enjoy being a parent. Waiting too long to have children has a downside, too. In my experience, waiting until there is reasonable certainty that the family can be stable is a good thing, and still being young enough to enjoy chasing after kids feels great. My wife and I switched roles early, as she worked a career while I went to graduate school and started a business. When we were more stable, I took the primary breadwinner role and she managed our young family. Two partners who can flex and work together to achieve good timing is a big advantage. When to have children? It's a major decision.

....

2 "The Motherhood Penalty vs. the Fatherhood Bonus," Claire Cain Miller, *The New York Times*, September 6, 2014, http://www.nytimes.com/2014/09/07/upshot/a-child-helps-your-career-if-youre-a-man.html

Decision Category: Our Social Circle

"We are an average of the five people

we spend the most time with."

—JIM ROHN

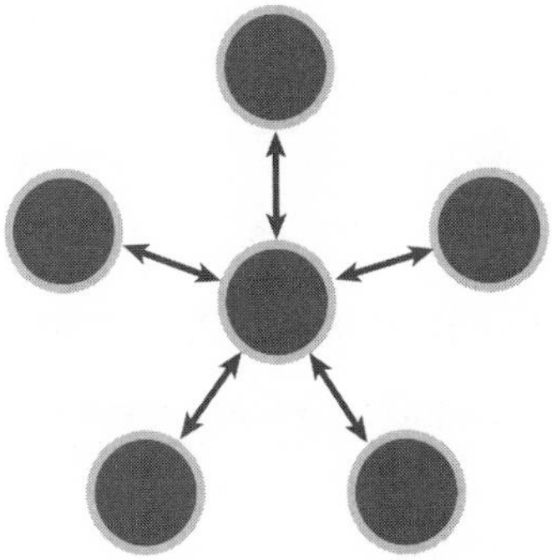

When it comes to the effects of relationships, we follow the law of averages. It turns out that we are greatly affected by the people closest to us. They affect how we think, how we feel about ourselves, and how we set goals and achieve. Think of the five people you spend the most time with. Do you like the effects of this group? Are you being challenged by the group, too?

It's important to have critics and advisors who don't always make us feel good. According to a study in the *Journal of Consumer Research*, "Tell Me What I Did Wrong: Experts Seek and Respond to Negative Feedback," novices have a preference for positive feedback, but experts want negative feedback so they can make progress.

And the more successful you become, the more criticism you'll face. Glenn Llopis at *Forbes* wrote about how "6 Types of People Build Your Mental Toughness," including doubters, critics, and the envious. These other actors in our life make us better. Your circle of closest people is a bigger decision than you may think.

Decision Category: Where we Live/Travel

Would you rather be a big fish in a small pond or a little fish in a big pond?

I would choose to start out in the big pond at all times. There is more opportunity, money, resources, brains, and talent (and spouse candidates) in the bigger pond. ***Where we live significantly affects opportunity.***

Talent and intelligence have been migrating to six major economic zones in the United States for the last one hundred years, leaving rural America and capitalizing upon competitive intensity. Locating within one of these zones will affect many of your opportunities:

- Northeast Corridor: Between Washington, DC and Boston
- Southeast: Between Virginia and Orlando, FL
- North-Central: Between Chicago and Minneapolis
- South-Central: Between Dallas, Houston, and San Antonio
- Pacific Northwest: Between Portland, OR and Seattle, WA
- West: California, from Los Angeles to San Francisco

These zones create more wealth and prosperity due to the more intense (due to population) collaboration of smart people to create new works. There are more people, investors, employers, brains, and talent for spontaneous combustion of ideas and opportunities.

On the other hand, you can live a happy life in the small pond, but you'll need to adjust your expectations and add travel. I live in a small pond—Tulsa, Oklahoma—by choice. But I travel frequently to the bigger ponds and work my opportunities. I travel abroad for exposure to what else the world is doing. I spend one week a month in large cities, working my network, seeing clients, and exploring my next opportunity. It's the best of both worlds, but I am certain it is more work to be highly successful while living in a small pond.

IN A LARGE POND, I HAVE FOUND THE FOLLOWING:

- More people, more people with talent/education, more traffic, painful commutes, dirtier air
- More opportunities, more things to do, higher cost of living, more budget pressure to work more hours instead of enjoying time off
- Many business relationships, many company headquarters located here
- Much easier travel by air, train, ride-sharing

IN A SMALL POND, I HAVE FOUND THE FOLLOWING:

- Lower cost of living
- Fewer opportunities, less to do
- Easier living, less congested, better air, people are less worldly

- Few business relationships; travel is a must
- Most trips include two flights each way

Decision Category: Career Choice and Income

In countries other than the United States, the career choice is not so democratic and flexible. To preserve scarce resources, other societies require testing and choices before the age of eighteen. In many European countries, you test at seventeen, and your advanced education (if any) and career path options are set for you before graduating high school. If you qualify, you can choose and are expected to not change your mind. If you aren't good enough, that's that.

Your career should provide income and fulfillment. Achieving great results for both factors is a challenge but also a thrilling pursuit. Your interests and joy in various types of work activities will help guide you to fulfilling work. From a decision-making standpoint, money is fuel for a great many other life goals, so we tend to choose income over fulfillment *or* fulfillment over income—and our goals must flip-flop accordingly. Fulfillment is often found by trying many jobs to discover what we absolutely don't like doing—and choosing from what remains.

Do you want to live comfortably? Your career will achieve or eliminate that goal. As examples, using the 50-30-20 budgeting rule in which 50 percent of income covers necessities, 30 percent is for discretionary items, and 20 percent is saved, following are single-person income requirements by city in 2016 to live comfortably (as surveyed by GOBankingRates):

City	Population	Annual Income Needed to Live Comfortably	Full-time Hourly Rate
New York	8,491,079	$87,446	$42
Los Angeles	3,928,864	$74,371	$36
Chicago	2,722,389	$68,671	$33
Houston	2,239,558	$60,795	$29
Philadelphia	1,560,297	$59,384	$29
Phoenix	1,537,058	$48,876	$23
San Antonio	1,436,697	$46,238	$22
San Diego	1,381,069	$69,307	$33
Dallas	1,281,047	$55,651	$27
San Jose, CA	1,015,785	$89,734	$43
Austin, TX	912,791	$53,225	$26
Jacksonville, FL	853,382	$49,842	$24
San Francisco	852,469	$119,570	$57
Indianapolis	848,788	$46,016	$22
Columbus, OH	835,957	$45,466	$22
Fort Worth, TX	812,238	$51,759	$25
Charlotte, NC	809,958	$53,842	$26
Detroit	680,250	$42,772	$21
El Paso, TX	679,036	$40,227	$19
Seattle	668,342	$72,092	$35
Denver	663,862	$62,842	$30
Washington, DC	658,893	$83,104	$40
Memphis, TN	656,861	$44,180	$21
Boston	655,884	$84,422	$41
Nashville, TN	644,014	$61,015	$29
Baltimore	622,793	$53,897	$26
Oklahoma City, OK	620,602	$44,180	$21
Portland, OR	619,360	$60,195	$29
Las Vegas	613,599	$50,453	$24
Louisville, KY	612,780	$46,831	$23
Milwaukee	599,642	$43,281	$21
Albuquerque, NM	557,169	$43,895	$21
Tucson, AZ	527,972	$39,966	$19
Fresno, CA	515,986	$42,496	$20

Continued

City	Population	Annual Income Needed to Live Comfortably	Full-time Hourly Rate
Sacramento, CA	485,199	$53,736	$26
Long Beach, CA	473,577	$58,560	$28
Kansas City, MO	470,800	$45,311	$22
Mesa, AZ	464,704	$42,654	$21
Atlanta	456,002	$60,285	$29
Virginia Beach, VA	450,980	$50,929	$24
Omaha, NE	446,599	$45,560	$22
Colorado Springs, CO	445,830	$44,512	$21
Raleigh, NC	439,896	$55,537	$27
Miami	430,332	$77,057	$37
Minneapolis	407,207	$64,170	$31
Cleveland	389,521	$42,589	$20
Wichita, KS	388,413	$40,616	$20

Your career will take you places. So, when moving from city to city, it's important to look up the difference in cost of living and make sure the income meets the needed budget.

One more point about career: What is the income range possible for your chosen work? As you advance in a career, low-income ceilings will cap your lifetime earning potential. Career considerations must include income ranges. Examples include (ninety percent of workers in each grouping fall inside the range shown)—

- Bartender/Waiter/Waitress: $12,500 – $28,200
- Janitorial Supervisor: $19,600 – $51,050
- Health Therapist: $20,900 – $72,600
- Registered Nurse: $40,200 – $83,400
- Technical Sales Representative: $33,400 – $121,800

- Financial Analyst: $40,300 – $130,100
- Computer Software Engineer: $49,400 – $119,800
- Physicist: $52,100 – $143,600
- Physician/Surgeon: $45,200 – $145,600

Harsh Reality:

Per the city income requirement illustration, above, when you see someone over the age of twenty-two and under the age of sixty-two working in a fast food restaurant or in the aisles of Walmart or in any other job with little upward income mobility that pays less than $20 per hour, you can be certain this person is under financial stress if they are living independently or have children to support. They are likely working two or three jobs to survive. I admire their hard work, but I also remind myself to make choices that allow me to never be in the same position.

Obviously, our decisions about education greatly impact career. These two decisions combine to set the income potential for most people.

Decision Category: Debt

Debt can be either good or bad. Debt is good when it is used to purchase an asset that will pay us to own it. Examples include rental property and businesses. Any debt undertaken in your name for anything that doesn't write you a check each month is bad debt.

One exception is debt incurred to pay for your education. That is an investment, if done wisely, in your future that will pay you back with a higher income range. Going into debt to buy a car, buy a house, buy "stuff," or to have a good time is baggage you must carry into the future. It can get heavy.

> **Nerd Wallet Report in 2015 AMERICAN HOUSEHOLD CREDIT CARD DEBT Study:**
> Why debt has grown: The rise in the cost of living has outpaced income growth over the past 12 years. While median household income has grown 26% since 2003, household expenses have outpaced it significantly—with medical costs growing by 51% and food and beverage prices increasing by 37% in that same span.

Nominal Income vs. Cost of Living

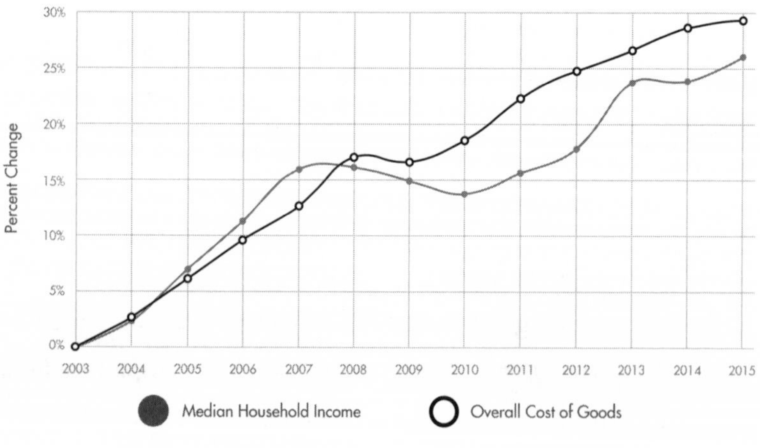

The psychology of debt: Consumers vastly underestimate or underreport how much debt they have. In fact, as of 2013, actual lender-reported credit card debt was 155% greater than borrower-reported balances.

The cost of debt: The average household is paying a total of $6,658 in interest per year. This is 9% of the average household income ($75,591) being spent on interest alone.[3]

The bottom line is: Taking on debt is a critical decision, and it is far too easy to get into trouble. Debt should be considered carefully when you contemplate how much freedom you want in your life.

Decision Category: Health and Lifestyle

"If you have your health, you have everything" is a traditional phrase. Americans and people in other developed nations are losing the wonderful health advantages we have developed because we are fat and getting fatter. Our daily decisions about our diet and lifestyle are failing us. Multiple rewards/penalties are due to our health and lifestyle choices. The greatest reward is a long, quality life. Every fast food burger, soft drink, and beer we consume is a decision toward heart disease and one that brings about the penalties in this decision category: society biases. Humans choose the fit and attractive partner, employers subconsciously choose the employee who best visually represents the company in addition to being qualified,

3 "2015 American Household Credit Card Debt Study," Erin El Issa, NerdWallet, December 9, 2015, https://www.nerdwallet.com/blog/credit-card-data/average-credit-card-debt-household/.

and weakness/feebleness is not a desirable trait in any competition. There is a natural bias against unfit and unhealthy people, and over half of us have lost control. Losing control lowers income.

Health: Are We Powerless?

More than two-thirds (70.7 percent) of adults are considered to be overweight or obese.

More than one-third (37.9 percent) of adults are considered to be obese. —CDC 2013–2014

Timothy A. Judge, from the University of Florida, and Daniel M. Cable, from the London Business School, set out to test the norms that society holds different body standards for men versus women by examining "the relationship between weight and income and the degree to which the relationship varies by gender." Here are some of their key findings:

> "For men, increases in weight have positive linear effects of pay but at diminished returns at above-average levels of weight." (Translation: Skinny men are at a disadvantage.)
>
> Note: *The Journal of Applied Psychology* found that men's muscles pay dividends:
>
> - "Studies have demonstrated that people assign positive personality traits to drawings or photographs of mesomorphic (muscular) men and mostly negative traits to

nonmesomorphic men. For example, traits ascribed to mesomorphic men were positive (i.e., best friend, has lots of friends, polite, happy, helps others, brave, healthy, smart, and neat). By contrast . . . ectomorphic (slender) men were described with a different set of negative traits (i.e., nervous, sneaky, afraid, sad, weak, and sick)."

- "Very thin" women earn approximately $22,000 more than their average-weight counterparts.
- "Thin" women earn a little over $7,000 more than their average-weight counterparts.
- "Heavy" women earn $9,000 less than their average-weight counterparts.
- "Very heavy" women earn almost $19,000 less than their average-weight counterparts.

What does this study tell us? It shows us that, as a society, our physical appearance is a key ingredient in workplace interactions, advancement, and personal income. To maximize income, it appears that men should hit the gym and pump iron, and women should stay proportioned so they look fit. Do I like this or agree with it? No. Some people have medical conditions that are irreversible. Bias doesn't care. We aren't going to change this bias overnight. You can try to change society's standards and make the bias less impactful. However, that may take many years. In the meantime, it is a punitive decision to ignore the disadvantages of appearing unfit and unhealthy. It's a significant decision on how we want to present ourselves to today's society.

Decision Category: Hobbies/Activities

What you do besides work and school makes you interesting. Elective pursuits are bonding topics, where you meet people and grow closer to them because of a shared passion for the activity. Common interests create friendships, romantic relationships, and new introductions. Biking, hiking, competitive shooting, tennis, church mission trips, volunteerism, antique collecting, travel, and bird watching are among thousands of common passions that can enrich your life. These activities open doors to the outside world.

Equally important is the aspect of challenging yourself in a hobby/activity as a life's pursuit. I have friends who are diligently working on their golf game. My mother has become an award-winning oil painter and she is working to become even better. It's a fun topic, competitive subject, and ever-challenging, mind-occupying obsession—to improve. That is good for us. It toughens us and keeps our competitive spirit alive, regardless of age. Our heart-pumping excitement toward our hobby carries over into our work and personal lives as we are stronger and thinking about our next milestone.

Decision Category: Lifetime Curiosity—Always Reaching, Learning, Finding New Ways to See the World

It is a decision to remain curious and continue learning throughout a lifetime. This decision takes over from your education growth decision when school is complete and lasts the rest of your life.

I have learned more from the follow-up question—because I was curious. I overcame my anxiety to talk to my future wife for the first time—because I was curious. I found a great mentor in graduate school—because I was curious. I got the promotion because I was curious enough to ask about the company's plans for the future. I learned new hobbies by trying new things with friends. To be curious is a state of mind, an interest in learning something new about someone or something. ***Curiosity opens unexpected doors.*** It is a lifelong asset to be curious.

One of the most reliable and overlooked keys to happiness is cultivating and exercising our innate sense of curiosity. That's because curiosity—a state of active interest or genuinely wanting to know more about something—creates an openness to unfamiliar experiences (adventure), laying the groundwork for greater opportunities to experience discovery, joy, and delight.

> *"Curiosity is something that can be nurtured and developed. With practice, we can harness the power of curiosity to transform everyday tasks into interesting and enjoyable experiences. We can also use curiosity to intentionally create wonder, intrigue and play out of almost any situation or interaction we encounter."*
>
> —TODD KASHDAN

It all starts with wanting to know more. It affects our lives in more ways than we can imagine. We can decide to be curious and follow the clues.

Decision Category: Choosing a Business Partner

If you are ever in business as an owner or co-owner, this area of decision making is critical. The most expensive lessons in my life have been due to poor choices in business partners. In fact, I lost more than $15 million dollars in 2010 in the demise of my manufacturing business because I was vulnerable to my partners and bankers. When things are going great, partners behave great. When things turn, you find out the truth. Business is hard enough without suffering from the self-serving whims or circumstances created by your business partner. Similar to choosing a spouse, a good business partner choice can mean 1+1=3. A bad business partner can kill your business and your bank account. There is not enough space in this book to cover every aspect of this decision category—but I wish to touch on my top principles.

DO YOU TAKE ON PARTNERS OR GO IT ALONE?

Business is more fun when you are not working alone, in my experience. The wonderful milestones, the victories, and the highs are all better when you can share them with a partner. The partner makes the lows more bearable as well. It's human nature. A partner adds capacity. People working together can make more discoveries and accomplish more. However, my partners have caused me the most grief in my life. That fact doesn't deter me from partnering—but I am now wiser when choosing! If an entrepreneur doesn't have the money to move a business forward, the answer is easy: He needs a partner with money. If that entrepreneur has enough money to conservatively make it work (but not quickly), he/she can go it alone, but the business will not scale quickly and it may lose its niche opportunity because demand doesn't wait for our businesses to grow. Demand will make someone else successful if we are not ready and able to grow. Partners can assist greatly with capital and/or effort. If you must have growth capital, there are only a few ways to acquire it. This was the reason I partnered with large capital sources (funds) and learned my painful $15 million lesson in partnering in 2010. We elevated the business value to new heights in 2008 and yet I was powerless to stop the carnage as it plummeted to earth a few years later due to errant decision making. In hindsight, the expression, "He who has the gold makes the rules" came to life before my eyes. When the shit hit the fan, nobody cared about partnership. Alternatively, magic can happen when partners come together. Steve Jobs and Steve Wozniak paired to create what would become Apple. Bill Gates and Paul Allen combined to create what would become Microsoft. We have all sent these companies a lot of money! So keep an open mind about partnership, and sparks can fly.

PARTNERSHIPS TURNING BAD

Once a partnership starts to sour for one of the partners, the bad behavior begins. I used to think that people were either good or bad and that would determine their behavior in the beginning, middle, and end of a partnership. Alternatively, while watching partnerships end, I have witnessed good people generate bad behavior toward their partner for common reasons:

- They feel the original business deal is now unfair.
- They feel they have been undercompensated (they are due).

- They feel their skills are undervalued by their partner.
- They feel hurt and want to inflict pain in return.
- They are kicking themselves for being so gullible.

We all know the feeling that comes over us when we know the partnership isn't going to last.

- Have you ever decided to fire an employee well ahead of their last day of work?
- Have you ever looked for a new romantic relationship while still holding on to the old one?
- Have you ever decided to make no further investment in a project or person well before telling anyone?
- Have you ever terminated a friendship but not told them?

Your behavior changes toward the other person under these circumstances, doesn't it? People's behavior in these scenarios includes hoarding ideas (not sharing), withholding information, creating side businesses, withholding time and energy, doing the minimum required to keep up appearances, etc.

Thus, when you think it might be going bad, trust your intuition. In business, you don't need anyone's blessing—just a good legal agreement. Spend the most energy picking your partners and less energy trying to hold something together that is flawed.

CHOOSING YOUR PARTNERS

My peers and I have agreed many times through the years (as we witnessed failure): ***The most important decisions we ever make in life are choosing our partners.*** Just look at how poorly some people choose their spouses. Many do an even worse job choosing whom they will marry in business. It turns out, divorce in marriage is usually much easier than unwinding business partnerships.

With a business partner, however, issues can originate from the partnership itself. Over time, your expectations can change. Your partner's work ethic can decline. Money can cause problems between you. Power is easily something to fight over. Second-guessing one another can become commonplace. Who is the real leader? Long-lasting partnerships in business are rare. I propose the primary reason for eventual dissolution is this: The differences between two partners in the beginning are complementary for the business—a balance of skills and perspective makes the business stable. However, as the business grows, some of those differences can become major disruptions. In the end, once both partners are financially stable, they will each place personal preferences ahead of tolerance and move along their own path. For years, I've noticed the tendency for married couples to drift apart. People change over time. Their relationships, wants, learning, energy, health, and spirit all combine to create a gradual drift away from their partner's. As I found out, choosing a business partner with whom you have no trusted background or relationship as well as having enormously greater capital will mean that you have very little say-so. Also, when partnering with a more powerful unknown, it is important to legally document your rights to prevent your "partner" from crashing your business because they are willing to risk what you are not. It reminds me of the story of the frog and the scorpion.

> In the story, a scorpion and a frog meet on the bank of a stream and the scorpion asks the frog to carry him across on its back. The frog asks, “How do I know you won’t sting me?” The scorpion says, “Because if I do, I will die too.” The frog is satisfied, and they set out, but in midstream, the scorpion stings the frog. The frog feels the onset of paralysis and starts to sink, knowing they both will drown, but has just enough time to gasp “Why?” Replies the scorpion: “It’s my nature.”

Thus, don’t choose to partner with a scorpion—regardless of what they promise. Your business partner needs to be someone you trust or someone who is legally bound to do the right thing else they lose and you do not. Partnership is strongest when the collective vision is clear, the motivations are the same, and the leverage is not one-sided. If you feel helpless in a partnership, it is not a partnership. Never take this partnership decision lightly. A friendship won’t survive a bad partnership, so proceed carefully and do so as if you are partnering with a stranger—so you have your eyes wide open for your decision making.

On this business partner topic, you are hopefully more aware now of the critical factor (good or bad) a partner can be in your success plan. This is not a definitive book on partnering, so please use my advice as basic caution to learn more when considering any type of partnership.

Decision Category: A Felony Conviction

Yes, it's a choice. This life-changing category almost didn't make the Biggie list and it would have been an unfortunate omission on my part. This is definitely the biggest category to avoid. I recently read Nicholas Eberstadt's book, *Men Without Work*, and I was floored to learn the odds of someone being unable to get a job are three times greater for someone convicted of a felony. In fact, there are at least twenty-three million felons in prime working age walking the streets right now, and their odds of success are permanently much lower for the rest of their lives. It doesn't matter if they made a simple mistake—they carry a permanent mark. And now they cannot work, marry, or start over—like the rest of us. Society doesn't want to look past a felony when offering opportunities. Single ladies don't want to tell mom and dad that their new beau is a felon.

Before you think, "Nah, no way this applies to me," let's look at how easy it is to get a felony on your record. As we look at this list, note how much stupidity can be fueled by alcohol and drugs. Felony convictions in America are most commonly earned for drug abuse/possession, property theft, driving under the influence (DUI), assault, buying alcohol for a minor, violent crimes, public drunkenness, burglary, vandalism, fraud, weapons violations, loitering, domestic violence, child abuse, possessing stolen property, and forgery. These aren't just crimes in dark alleys by experienced criminals. Most felons had one single decision go very bad. It's the drunk college student or the angry boyfriend or the desperate addict. It could easily be you tomorrow if you are put in the right circumstances without a clear mind.

It occurs to me that the Biggie decision category "Our Social Circle" can have a great impact upon keeping us out of trouble or getting us into this Felony category. Keep your eyes on the prize and don't play with fire by hanging around those who do. So for this category, being aware to never cross this line is valuable knowledge. A felony can impact everything you ever wanted and leave you powerless to overcome its effects.

·4·

THE DECISION ZONES

For decisions, how or why we make mistakes is less important than *when* we make mistakes. In other words, bad decisions made at a vulnerable time create maximum damage. In life, Decision Zones are meaningful to our personal success. I have seen friends as well as my children navigate these zones blindly, unaware that they have crossed from one zone to the other. The key is to be aware of these zones and the incredible power they have in our total life.

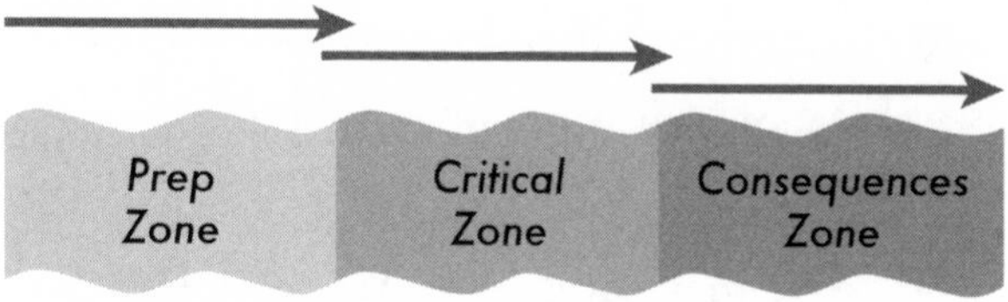

Imagine you are a jet fighter pilot and your aircraft is parked on the tarmac. You approach it on a mission. Your first order of business has been to prepare your abilities, taking years to accomplish, as well as to prepare for this particular flight. You inspect the aircraft, running your hand along its sleek body. Is it ready for action? Are you armed for the mission? You are leaving the Prep Zone.

You begin your takeoff and your adrenaline flows. The test of all your preparation begins as you go "wheels up." You've entered the Critical Zone. You burn a lot of fuel to get airborne. You reach a cruising altitude and let out a deep breath. You are a young pilot, and this is the career you wanted. You are in formation with other pilots, working together, at cruising speed.

Suddenly, your radar begins beeping, and unknown aircraft approach. You dive low to remain unseen, the trees coming so close you can count them. Other pilots are yelling on the intercom as you must maintain your cool and decide what to do, which bogey to follow. Do you engage? Do you ignore? Are you under threat? Watch out for the ground below. So many decisions now. Sweat beads form on your face as you are suddenly overloaded with information and your body begs for extra time to process it all. Aircraft swirl, and the airspace is suddenly crowded and deadly serious. You are missing the training days of preparation because it is all suddenly so real.

What you do now is critical. One wrong move can lead to a demotion and loss of your wings or even death for you and your peers. Finally, based upon your training, judgment, and instinct, you act. The act cannot be undone. You've entered the Consequences Zone. Only the consequences of your act can happen now. The effects smoothly land you back to earth intact with your squad mates and a smile on your face ("mission accomplished") or, alternatively, you crash and burn, creating permanent damage in your life to you, your future, and/or others you care about. The mission (as you intended it) has failed. These are real consequences and they remain forever. Let's look at the zones closely.

What Is the Prep Zone?

"Prep" is all the work you and your parents attempt up until the age where you have the steering wheel to your life and it's up to you to "make it." The age range is generally ten to sixteen years where study habits are formed and carried out, work ethic is formed, and a sense of who we want to be is crafted. Preparation can extend into adulthood, of course. Yet we all grow up urgently wanting to finally make decisions for ourselves. If we only knew how safe the Prep Zone was compared to the Critical Zone!

What Is the Critical Zone?

The twelve Biggie decision categories discussed in chapter 3, incredibly, get the most activity between the ages of sixteen and forty. These Biggies are Critical because the results tend to be big and impact you forever. This is the core time span of self-directed life, love, experiences, adventures, strategy, and deal making. That's a twenty-four-year window of time in which the average person sets up their entire life to achieve their personal definition of success. In hindsight, these years go by too fast, and I wish I had read this book at sixteen. You don't have to be perfect in this zone, but you've got to be careful. You will lose lifetime momentum and opportunity if you choose poorly.

What Is the Consequences Zone?

Just as the name suggests, these are the fifty-plus years (the majority of your life) where you get to enjoy the fruits of decisions made in the Critical Zone. Alternatively, some people must carry the burden instead (the "consequences"). "Happily married," adequate income, retirement savings, travel, grandchildren, etc. are some good examples of positive consequences.

The Saddest Man I Ever Met

As I asked friends for stories of the Consequences Zone, a college friend shared a personal story: "At the age of thirty-three, I met my biological father for the first time. He was fifty-four. It was a nervous meeting. He had a kind face. He had chosen to not be a part of my life since before I was born. Curiosity couldn't keep me away forever—even though I hated him for his decision about me years ago. Beyond initial small talk, I quickly saw the man was drowning in regret. He was alone in the prime of his life. He had worn through two marriages and several children. He was broke. He drove an old car and made money working odd jobs. His kids didn't talk to him much. He could only talk about what he used to have and used to do. He used to manage a business, used to make money, used to write, used to talk and people would listen. Now there was only yesterday's pride and today's resentment of others. He didn't feel respected. He had made bad decisions his entire life. The consequences were crushing. It was a stunning display of something I never wanted to be: full of scorned pride masking massive regret that he could not fully stomach, so he blamed people he used to love. He was the saddest man I ever met."

Decision Zones and The Young Adult

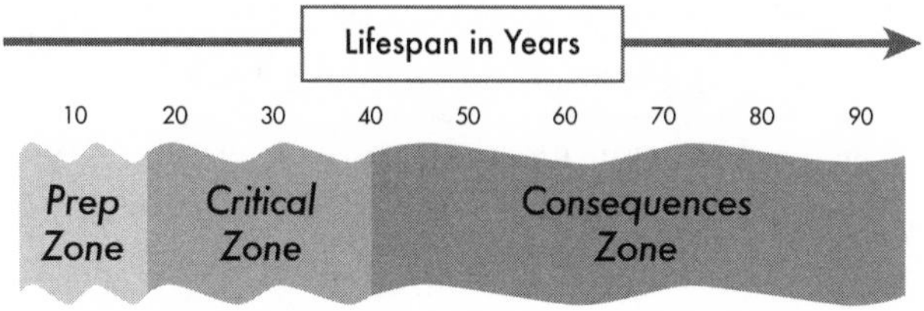

Hey, teenager or young adult, you are the envy of the rest of us. You have two things we wish we had: (1) lots of time; (2) a clean slate/record so far in life. You are getting older with a lot of new responsibility. Yet before we all take off in our lives (leaving home, going to college, going rogue), we do the work and preparation our parents and our schools and advisors require of us. This work is for our own good and it isn't all fun. We parents and advisors demand preparation from young people, but we don't do a good job explaining why. The young adult simply sees and feels the work now—not the future effects they cannot see or touch. It's difficult to convince someone to prepare for the unknown (e.g., the value of avoiding regret when they have never really encountered it). It's like preparing to survive an earthquake when only slight tremors have been their experience. The youthful perspective cannot fully go there into the hypothetical, and that is what frustrates us adults. We just want you to believe us because we have your best interests at heart. Yes, serious consequences are possible due to bad decisions, and we wish we could help you avoid finding out how bad they can be. Also, before anyone exclaims, "It's good to learn from mistakes!" let me clarify to the young, upstart person: Learning is good, but there are

Biggie Decisions in the Critical Zone that you will value or regret for the rest of your life. If you want your freedom in your future years and you want to do a lot of things and travel to a lot of places and accomplish big feats, you must set up the Critical Zone correctly. If you do it right, the Consequences Zone is a friend for the rest of your life. My brother, for example, made his Critical Zone decisions well. I am proud of him as he is enjoying his Consequences Zone. His secret in the Preparation and Critical Zones was likely doing the opposite of his older brother (me).

AN IDEAL (NORMAL) TIMELINE:

You learn, you make the big decisions, and then you enjoy the fruits of those early decisions the rest of your life.

Testimonial 1
(Nineteen-year-old Male; College Sophomore)

I had no idea there were so many decisions ahead of me. I worked hard in high school and tried to get into the best college that fit me. It is intimidating to think that my decisions over the next ten years can make or break my future happiness. I know it is not that black/white, but the idea of the Critical Zone has been a wake-up call for me. My friends have no idea about these concepts and I see them taking many risks. I am now looking at the sizes of decisions and I am extra careful with the big decisions. I am most fearful of regretting my choices as I get older. I am undecided for my desired degree, so that decision will be one of the big decisions I will try to make in the next year.

Testimonial 2 (Fifty-two-year-old Married Female with Two Children; Airline Industry Professional)

As the middle daughter of two career professionals, I learned early to work hard. I went to college to be an aeronautical engineer. I sat in classes surrounded by males thinking I could do anything they could and I was going to pave my way up the corporate ladder. Then it happened, in my collegiate senior year, pregnant!

Life made a sharp turn. I had made a mistake and now my next decision was critical. I decided my baby was priority #1 and left school with only a few classes short of a college degree. It was a daunting turn down an unexpected path. It was very humbling, and my future was forever changed. Eventually I joined a global airline, and after years of working hard was nominated by my peers to be an inaugural member of the Chairmen's Club recognizing the top one hundred employees out of fifty thousand. I may not have had the framed diploma on the wall or distinguished title on my business card, but I had found my own path to the top!

I regret not finishing my college degree. The impact of not completing my degree was far greater than I ever would have imagined. My company eventually implemented a policy for promotion within the company. A degree was required—which I did not have.

Upon leaving the company, a college degree was important in my new work search. I had my award recognition and work experience to help, but there were positions I wanted that I could not get without the degree. With the degree I would have advanced my career faster, with higher compensation, and would be in the position to buy a home or more ably save for retirement.

Continued

Having children in your early twenties is tough financially without savings to lean on. It's the most significant decision and it changed the course of my life and expectations. The big win alternatively is being able to enjoy my kids and grandkids while still young and active. It only takes one little smile from my grandchildren and I know the "life" degree was the perfect path for me.

Decision Zones and The Midlife Adult (The Big Reset)

If you're like my brilliant brother and have only made great decisions so far in life, you can move beyond this section—but there is still a lot of time left and you never know what will happen tomorrow. As I look around at my peers, it is clear, frankly, that many of us screw up in the first half of our life. It's common. Perhaps you have one or more of the following situations:

- Divorce/split family
- Failed business
- Too reliant upon someone else (held hostage)
- Failure to meet the right person
- Not enough education or skills to qualify for better paying work
- Didn't take care of my health and now it is affecting everything I do
- Little/no savings
- Jail, bankruptcy, drug use
- Derailed by the actions of someone else

So what do we do about it now? Regardless of what happened in the past, we still have dreams and goals we want to accomplish—but how do we recover? How do we make our prior years' hard lessons work constructively for us going forward? The answer is: We must do The Big Reset. It may be scary to admit that The Big Reset is necessary in your life. This step can be taken at any time, and it requires honesty, clarity, and a belief that you can do better going forward. You simply decide to reset. It will sometimes feel unsteady and it should feel challenging—because you want to make an important change in the middle of your life: transforming from victim of your past to director of your future. During this Big Reset, you must be brave and committed. Involve your closest friends in your efforts. Their support will be reassuring.

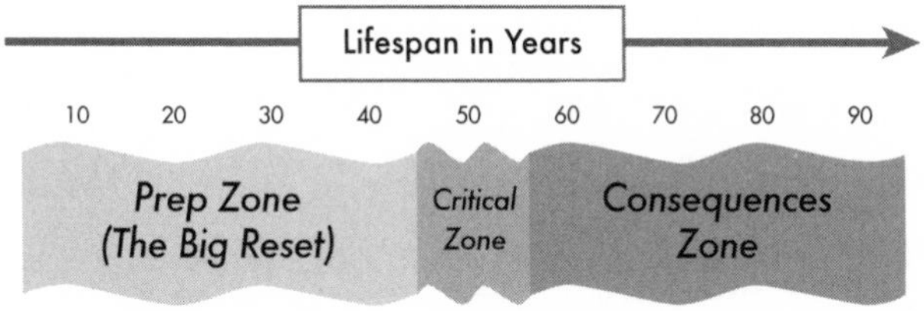

The Big Reset is a fresh approach to the rest of our life, and the sooner we do it, the sooner we benefit. A reset midlife changes the Decision Zone picture. Experiences are shuffled and time is compressed, starting now. In The Big Reset, all our pre-reset years are thrown into the Prep Zone, and the next ten years are the Critical Zone, regardless of our age. We have to stop kicking ourselves over anything concerning our new expanded Prep Zone and simply use those years as support for what's next—and how we want to remake ourselves and our future. We use that wisdom as past "prep," and we go forward with a revised definition of success for our lives. (Do you see how important that conversation about "success" is becoming?) Starting on the day of the reset, we use the next ten years to make great decisions. This compresses the zones, but it is a positive way to deal with the past (finito!) and start fresh. One huge point to understand is that our starting point is where we are today, with all assets and blemishes, and progress will begin here, not from somewhere in our past.

A BIG RESET TIMELINE:

You learn, you make the big decisions, you relearn, repair, and restart, and then you enjoy the fruits of the reset decisions the rest of your life.

Testimonial 1 (Forty-eight-year-old Married Male with Three Children; Entrepreneur; Writer)

Your humble author did The Big Reset in 2012 after a dismal 2009–2011 period of time for my business (also my largest investment). A bad partner choice combined with the Great Recession and a struggling bank led to a business failure. Fifteen years of hard work as an entrepreneur and millions of dollars went up in smoke. Failure had incredible power to gut-punch my psyche, call into question my state of mind, create infinite opportunities to second-guess myself, and assign blame. Ultimately, the whole mess required my financial restart—a forced restart for someone who plans everything for success but didn't have control in this case. I just had to sit there and take it. As an entrepreneur since I graduated college, I couldn't instantly start a business in a whole new industry and have it cover the expenses of my growing family. It was a tough time and I went through a reset but didn't realize it until later.

So, in The Big Reset, I finally quit kicking myself and mourning my former wealth and pride in my business, and I focused upon myself—what I am, what I do well, what makes me who I am, and how that creates value for other people. Here is what I did.

I introduced myself to humility. Yes, I got really humble. Failure has a way of doing that to us. Part of this process included me forgiving myself—accepting that I wasn't perfect and the world wasn't going to be perfect, either. While I was probably overconfident before, I was much more reserved in how I saw myself and my achievements. In the end, humility has been very healthy—for me.

I got closer to the things that really mattered to me: my family, a few friends, my health, and a hobby (trapshooting).

I moved all my life lessons to my past, placing them in the Prep Zone.

I adjusted my spending harshly so I wouldn't have to worry as much about income as I was starting my next venture. Things can always be upgraded and downgraded.

I focused upon creating something of lasting value—something that got me excited. I polished my ability to turn my best ideas into real products and businesses.

I created a new set of decision-making principles—because I had some catching up to do in my life plan. Many of these tools are in this book.

People have asked me: "If you could go back in time and relive your Critical Zone, would you avoid doing this Big Reset?" In my case, I would not because it changed what I value and who I am and what I think is important. We cannot go backward, so we go forward and turn this into an opportunity. I am convinced that The Big Reset can be a wonderful transition in our life's journey.

Testimonial 2 (Fifty-year-old Divorced Female; No Children; Entrepreneur)

When my business closed, I felt my boat of security had been tipped over and I was caught in the rapids. There was chaos, confusion, and a loss of direction. My initial instinct was to panic and start grabbing for anything or anyone that looked or felt solid. Then I stopped myself, took a deep breath, and started to look beyond the easiest and most familiar solution (to keep doing what I had always done). I began to evaluate my current situation by asking myself, What were the good decisions I made? What where the bad ones? Which ones could I let go of? Which ones could I use to leverage my future? Was this raging river I found myself in as deep and dangerous as it felt in that moment of panic? Had I really examined the river's depth? Perhaps all I needed to do was simply stand up! Or perhaps floating downstream for a while would allow me to see better options.

My thoughts began to drift away from what my job should be to what my life should be. My current career (or lack of one) was stressing me out. So after evaluating what I loved—and what I didn't love—about it, I discovered countless areas of opportunity that would allow me to utilize my past experience and expertise without having to stay in the same disappointing work. I saw my future as much more than just a job or a title. I wanted a better life!

Once I focused on dividing my past choices in life as good decisions or bad decisions, it was much easier to focus on my current situation in the same way. Is it a good decision to panic? Is it a good decision to slow down and think for a few days before repeating my bad habits?

Hitting the "reset" button for me meant finding my flow, taking my focus off of "finding a new job," and instead focusing on finding opportunities that checked the boxes on my joy list. It meant reevaluating where I was spending my time (at more productive networking events or with friends that increased—rather than depleted—my energy) and reevaluating my career (finding other ways to consult, be creative, share knowledge). Once I realized which decisions I had made that were not serving me well, I was able to start making decisions that would serve me well—which led to some significant changes in my life almost immediately.

Big Reset Insurance

If we don't want to be forced to do The Big Reset in our future, then we must master the decisions made in the Critical Zone the first time we encounter them. Doing well with the concepts in this book will prevent the need to ever do The Big Reset. From interviews of my middle-aged peers, most "resetters" believe it was only a couple big decisions made in their Critical Zone that they wish they could take back. They value decision-making discipline now because they hurt themselves—but they didn't respect it earlier in their lives. This is exactly the mindset I am trying to change. That is what I am telling my children today.

The Brutal Odds

"Somebody's gotta win and somebody's gotta lose and I believe in letting the other guy lose."

—PETE ROSE

As in every contest, a winner emerges from the rest of the pack. Thus, if every competitor of yours today is good at decision making, your path in life will be a lot harder. Not everyone can optimize their life's decisions to achieve goals they want. Most people tend to "settle" for where they end up. You can always settle for less than you originally wanted. I think you can do better. Let's look further.

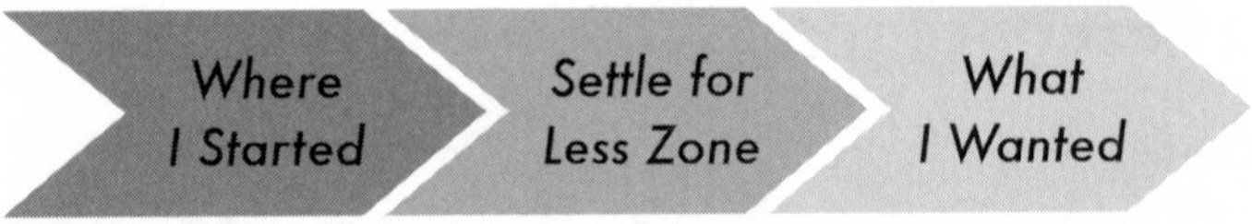

What does our society reward? Who gets into the best schools? Who gets the lead role? Who gets the valuable internship, the job, the promotion? Who gets chosen?

The answer is: The person who best fits the chooser's desires.

Thus, what do people generally desire?

The answer is: What is rare, exceptional, enjoyable, or valuable.

So, what can we conclude about the general nature of decision making when we are trying to beat the odds (in competition with other people for what we want)?

The answer is: Decisions about ourselves should help us be more rare, exceptional, enjoyable, or valuable.

We are exploring beating the competition in pursuit of what you want. Everyone is doing the same for themselves. Winning is reaching your definition of success: success for today, this month, next year, and a lifetime. You decide what a win looks like.

In the past, I resented people who were given things as a head start. I felt like they were unfairly getting better odds of success. How can the guy at state college compete with the fellow whose parents could afford Ivy League schools? As I met more peers who were given larger early advantages, it became clear to me that their odds of getting a higher-paying situation were better, but their odds of being successful were possibly the same as or less than mine. This is because I realized "success" is not my bank account or paying high property taxes on a large home, or working sixty-plus hours per week. What makes people "successful" is happiness. Happiness is people feeling good about their dreams and the decisions they make achieving those dreams. When they have both, they tend to be successful. So, regardless of where you and I started, our odds of success are even greater if we apply this language of decision making to our lives.

PERSONAL EXERCISE:
Biggie Decision Inventory

Complete this quick exercise, listing the most significant decision you can recall so far in your life in the Biggie categories. Remember a big decision can be to choose to either *do* or *not do* something. For this important exercise, please make a handwritten response. Perhaps use a separate sheet of paper to record your thoughts.

Dated as of ____/____/________

Decision Category: Education

My biggest decision so far has been:

____

Decision Category: Whom to Take as Life Partner and When

My biggest decision so far has been:

____

Decision Category: Having Children and When

My biggest decision so far has been:

____

Decision Category: Our Social Circle

My biggest decision so far has been:

____

Decision Category: Where We Live/Travel

My biggest decision so far has been:

____

Decision Category: Career Choice and Income

My biggest decision so far has been:

____

Decision Category: Debt

My biggest decision so far has been:

____

Decision Category: Health and Lifestyle

My biggest decision so far has been:

____

Decision Category: Hobbies/Activities

My biggest decision so far has been:

____

Decision Category: Lifetime Curiosity

My biggest decision so far has been:

____

Decision Category: Choosing a Business Partner

My biggest decision so far has been:

____

Decision Category: Avoiding a Felony Conviction

My biggest decision so far has been:

____

•5•

DECISIONS DEFINE US

If we take the role of poor decision maker for the moment, then, by comparison, who are the good decision makers? Imagine that you are attending a large party of people, the majority unfamiliar to you, and you are looking for good decision makers. How do you find them? As you look around the room, examining each person, it could easily be a masquerade party with every face in disguise. The outer appearance says little about the decisions that bring us to this moment. Yet, the party is full of good and bad decision makers. How can we tell?

I'll answer that question with another question: What is the trait that creates an "I met this great guy/gal?" reaction? This feeling comes after some conversation, of course. In the words shared, what was communicated by each of us that is measurable? I suggest that the questions we ask while making small talk prompt answers that provide important clues about someone's decision-making track record. Did you realize that you are actually interviewing other people about their track record?

"What do you do?"—Shows career and education decisions, and status on career ladder (simultaneously calculating their age to test how swiftly they advanced)

"Where are you from?"—Shows where they started and clarifies how far they have traveled since (simultaneously calculating their age to test how swiftly they advanced)

"**What are your interests?"**—Shows their decisions to be worldly, well-rounded, competitive, or lifetime learner

"Who are your friends?"—Shows to whom they relate and gives you live, animated decision-making evidence for what they value and how they spend their time

"How do you spend money?"—This is a silent question that reveals decisions galore. The answers come with their appearance, stories, and color commentary about their lives.

The questions they ask you—Ah ha! This wasn't a one-sided conversation with a wall. Our ears are tuned to the questions they ask us. The questions tend to indicate what they value. If they discuss deep subjects, they are deep or analytical and comfortable with the conversation. If they discuss weather and Twitter, they are keeping the conversation light. The logical or organized way in which someone asks us questions is revealing, and the details tell you what they value.

Confidence—We always react positively to the person with "quiet confidence"—a more subtle, not-trying-too-hard-to-impress, content-with-myself demeanor when put in the position to sink or swim in front of a stranger. It's a nonverbal dictionary on display. Very simply, quiet confidence is hard to fake. Thus, the confidence you observe, if real, is due to their personal report card at this moment—and that is based upon the grade they assign themselves for their decision making and results right now.

Imagine you are leaving that party and are summarizing what you have learned about the people you encountered. You have a quick sense of whether a person is skillful in their decision making. Trust your gut feelings because your mind is adding this up all the time. Question: If you met yourself at this party, would you evaluate yourself as a good decision maker?

Why Do I Care Who the Good Decision Makers Are?

"Luck is not as random as you think.

Before that lottery ticket won the jackpot, someone had to buy it."

—VERA NAZARIAN, *THE PERPETUAL CALENDAR OF INSPIRATION*

You care who the good decision makers are because you want to be one! In every group, the good decision makers stand out. They are good bets. They make good partners. They have done more with less, in less time than everyone else. They have better feel-good, motivational stories. They attract a crowd by their *progress*, not their public relations.

Uniquely Me

Our lives are not comparable to anyone else's life because we started from different places and have had different experiences every day since. We have different personalities, values, resources, and desires. Thus, I cannot walk down the shopping aisle of the virtual grocery store and purchase "Happiness" or "Fulfillment" or "Thrilling" or "Challenged" or "Educated" or "Rich" from the available products. There is not a prepackaged plan we can adopt that will get us where we want to be. We only have the ingredients of our own lives with which we can learn to cook for ourselves. This approach doesn't require luck, and the odds are excellent in your favor—because you know yourself and you have more control than you may think.

"I've Got This"—The Four Self-Coaching Points

1. We are living and directing our own life, and that cannot be accurately compared to someone else. They were born different than us, began with different circumstances, and it is unfair to our psyche to constantly be comparing ourselves to others.
2. Progress today is measured by where we were yesterday, not measured by comparing ourselves to someone else or society's expectations.
3. We are continually getting better at managing ourselves and our future. If we are observant and avoid being prideful, we will improve.

4. You can only trust your own instincts on what works for you. All other opinions must be discounted because they do not have your perspective or risks.

If you will embrace the above four precepts for coaching your life, you will see the power of the following exercise. Let's do this!

An Illustration: Cooking Up Success with Decisions

Imagine you are the chef and you are in charge of your only creation, soup. You make the decisions. The ingredients you have available to put into the soup come from these categories (reflect on the ingredients you have available today in these categories):

- What God gave you
- What your parents gave you
- What you have learned as of today
- What you have collected on your own
- What you have created on your own
- The opportunities that are in front of you

How would you know how great soup tastes? How will you know when you've reached success? Ask yourself, what should a successful soup taste like? If you have tasted it before, you'll remember it. However, if you have not, you must be aware of the goal. If you can detail your expectations, you will avoid experimenting endlessly in life and know success when you see it. You need to know how you want it to taste when you are done.

An awareness of your inventory is critical before attempting this soup. Do you lack an essential ingredient? If so, how can you obtain it so you have that ingredient available when you need it? If you are missing an essential ingredient, like tomatoes for tomato soup, you will need to be realistic and choose a different soup to make.

It makes no sense to discuss or covet someone else's ingredients because they don't apply to you. If you like what someone else is putting in his soup, you must figure out how to obtain that ingredient yourself. Realism is helpful here. In fact, it lets you off the hook in a way. Realities such as

"I don't have Brad Pitt's looks, so I need to use the face I have."

"I don't have the money for an Ivy League education,
so I need to get the best education I can afford."

"I didn't invent Facebook, but I need to invent something."

"I have a natural talent for selling, so I need to put it to use."

"I want to be an entrepreneur but don't know how;
I'd better find out how."

Don't spoil the soup! Once you add an ingredient, you cannot take it out, right? A poor decision can spoil the soup, and fixing this batch is not always possible. If spoiled, The Big Reset may be required—which we want to avoid because it is costly and takes extra time.

So what are the traditional cooking decisions that tend to ruin soup-making effort? (Keep your life in mind as you read.)

- Too much of any ingredient that unbalances the taste (e.g., salt)
- Failure to have the ingredients we need when we need them
- Boiling the soup (and the chef with it)
- Other cooks whom we trusted that we shouldn't have trusted
- Making the wrong soup

KNOW WHEN IT'S TIME TO START OVER WITH NEW SOUP

No amount of spice can overcome bad soup. At some point, regardless of your investment, the soup must be tossed and we start over. This applies to careers, relationships, and homemade cookies. When you detect that it cannot be saved, make the right call. Start over.

HOW DO WE KNOW WE ARE GREAT CHEFS WITH THIS SOUP?

Answer 1: Did we do the best with the ingredients we had?

Answer 2: Are we satisfied with and willing to eat our own cooking?

The Decision Streak

DEFINITION: Winning Streak–

A series of consecutive successes, a run of good luck

In sports, a winning streak refers to a consecutive number of games won. A winning streak can be held by a team, as in baseball, football, basketball, or hockey, or by an individual.

The concept of a winning streak in terms of decision making is a "Decision Streak." ***For decisions, it's about putting together a series of good decisions, one after another, like a hitting streak for a baseball player.*** With every decision in the streak, the next one becomes more important—because the momentum for you builds . . . and you notice the dividends of a streak.

A Professional Baseball Hitter's Challenge

Over the course of a season, the difference between batting .250 and .300 is only one more hit a week! That could be a "ground ball with eyes" or a bloop over the first baseman's head! More importantly and perhaps even easier is making one or two fewer outs a week by not swinging at bad pitches.

The hitter is making decisions! Only one more good decision a week puts the player under a multimillion dollar contract vs. in danger of going to the minor leagues or being cut. One more hit a week—via a good decision!

A hitter on a "streak" is hot because they are in a groove in their decision making and their form. Even on days they don't feel perfect, they still hit because the opposing pitcher cannot outwit the hitter's decision-making discipline. Tricks don't work. Fundamentals and mental discipline win most of the time.

Perhaps we can do better in our decisions if we remember clearly the "good pitch we are looking for" and see clearly and avoid the bad pitches. What confidence that can bring!

Career Example of a Common Decision Streak

Do you go to a work function with a friend? It's boring, but you might meet someone interesting.

Decision: I'll go.

At the work function, do you introduce yourself to strangers and strike up conversations or do you stay mostly quiet? Strangers can bring new surprises and opportunity.

Decision: Strike up conversations.

One of the people you meet is listing a job in a field you find somewhat interesting. Do you apply? If you apply, you have a chance at a new opportunity.

Decision: Apply.

You were offered the job. Do you take it? Your Decision Streak delivered this opportunity to take the new job. Does the Decision Streak continue and you accept the new job?

So, three small decisions led to one big decision. The big decision would have never happened if you hadn't respected the value of a Decision Streak. Some options are only revealed after the first decision is made. Simply staying focused upon making the best decision, choosing well from the available options, will bring you the best outcomes that were ever possible.

Have you ever hit multiple green lights in a row while driving downtown? What efficiency! Decision Streaks feel the same way and create winning momentum. Deciding to go to the gym every day can create winning momentum toward your fitness goal. Deciding to learn something new is the first step toward being someone new. Successful people tend to put together Decision Streaks, and they expect those streaks to continue—because they have gotten used to the streak and they highly value the results it brings.

Exponential Effects of Decisions

"It's so important to know where you are. I know where I am right now. How do you go from where you are to where you want to be? I think you have to have an enthusiasm for life. You have to have a dream, a goal. You have to be willing to work for it."

—JIM VALVANO

Two former high school classmates see each other for the first time in twenty years at a class reunion. They were raised in the same town, with similar parents, same high school, same education, similar grades, and similar goals. After twenty years, one classmate talked excitedly about her life and prospects for the future while the second classmate listened distantly and could only wish she could be speaking in such terms. Why would that be? Most likely, the only reason they differ today is due to a Decision Streak for one of them and not the other. In twenty years, the quantity and quality of decision making and resulting experiences made a dramatic impact upon their lives.

The stories come from everywhere. Some people get "lucky" and others have to work harder. In fact, hard work includes careful thought. In the end it is undeniable that a series of great decisions is the big difference maker between those who consider themselves successful and those who do not. The effects upon happiness, satisfaction, income, health, and life flexibility are exponential—when a decision is well made. So, regardless of where you started or where you are today, *you* can create a streak of winning decisions. Did you know that your first success decision is reading this book?

Luck and Deceit

I am driving down the highway, minding my own business. As I pass a semitruck in the next lane, it starts moving over into my lane. Uh oh. The driver doesn't see me. I am not going to slow this giant machine down if it wants to move my car over, so I have a choice: Speed up or slow down—but deal with it *now*. Like this truck, there are two things we encounter in life, and we cannot choose when they occur and must deal with them: *luck* and *deceit*.

When good luck shines upon us, it is wonderful but it is also random. Our decisions *after* experiencing good luck are the key to using luck to power our momentum forward in life. Luck can be exponentially powerful. Unfortunately, humans are generally terrible with decisions after luck blesses them. Look at the track record of most lottery winners for proof that decisions post-luck are incredibly important. When we recognize luck, we need to save it, preserve it, like a fresh-cut flower. It may last only a day. In this mindset, we put the benefits in the bank or use the luck as a ladder to climb higher. Put the luck to work. That is a decision.

On the other hand, another thing we cannot control are people's intentions. People will lie to us. We cannot control their motives or their honesty. Like luck, once we have evidence of deceit, we have a decision to make. We must become less vulnerable to this person. We learn over time to detect deceit in deeds, words, and body language. Yet love and hope and greed can blind our senses where we miss the clues. On deceit, trust your instincts. There is nothing more accurate than human instincts when sniffing out deceit. Deceit happens and we can make a decision to move forward correctly. Sometimes, moving forward requires recovery—but that is still moving forward.

Deceit is in the eyes of the deceiver. Why else have professional poker players resorted to wearing sunglasses at the poker table to hide their eyes? Little things like normal eye contact, looking away, squints, winks, and focus are changed when someone is full of BS. I meet face-to-face whenever I am discussing/negotiating the bigger points to any deal. If I cannot meet with the other party in the same room, we have a telephone call. I listen for voice inflection (stress), pauses, and emotions (anger, indifference, flippancy). I need every clue I can collect. However, I've noticed that email and texting removes our eyes and our ears from two important areas of instinctual programming: watching and listening to the other person. Email, social media posts, and texts are carefully massaged communications—so don't rely upon them to judge someone. Get your eyes and ears tuned in to the people to whom you are vulnerable. The next good decision is to move away from this newly discovered vulnerability before it does further damage in our lives. And if this is your second or third reminder and you didn't listen before, do yourself a favor and take action.

·6·

WHAT WE DO WRONG

Now that we have recognized the incredible significance decisions have in our lives and we can clearly see that we are in charge of our own success, let's make a solid effort to identify how we humans get decisions wrong so we can put those habits in our past and finish strong with a new game plan. Let's examine the nature of how our bad decision-making process happens.

The Next Step

Secretly, we tell ourselves that we are good decision makers, don't we? How did your self-interview work out as you judged your past decision making? In reality, all of us are bad decision makers sometimes, but the quantity and type of decision-making errors separate the good from the bad decision makers. Let's dig into the nature of the bad decision maker!

Naturally Wrong, Part 1—The Missing Link Called "Why"

"The presence of a path doesn't necessarily mean the existence of a destination."

—CRAIG D. LOUNSBROUGH

The most common failure in decision making is making a choice based upon how we *feel* instead of *why* this particular choice gets us closer to what we want in life. How we feel is a bad why. ***A goal is a good why.*** The *goal* is the thing we want, the object of our pursuits. It has been planted in our brains by our interests, observing others, or by people suggesting to us what to do.

COMMON GOALS

- "I want him/her"
- "I want to go to this school"
- "I want this new car"
- "I want this degree"
- "I want this job"
- "I want this opportunity"
- "I want to move to this city"
- "I want more freedom"
- "I want more income"

The Why

It's amazing to me how little people consider the big picture "why" when they are making a decision, deciding upon an action. I believe this happens for these reasons: (1) the instant gratification is easier to identify than the long-term benefits or consequences; and (2) their goals are not clear so they cannot test against those goals.

The "why" is our motivation and justification for choosing this "action." The why should fit within our success path, accomplishing our goal. It's an easy question: "Will this choice get me what I want?" *Why* we are doing something is more important than anything. The consequences of doing something without thinking about why can be catastrophic.

COMMON VALID WHYS

- "Because this helps me achieve a goal I have"
- "Because this is good for me"
- "Because this is part of the journey to where I want to go"
- "Because it is the proper/kind thing to do for someone else"

The Good, The Bad

The simple failure to connect your "action" to your "why" in decision making is a huge error in connecting your immediate present to your better future. It's connecting the dots to what you want! If you want marriage, why are you dating someone who is completely not partner material? If you don't want to advance in the profession you are currently working, why are you in this job? If you don't really want something, why are you trying so hard to do it?

Even more simply, if our success definition entails us dropping twenty pounds, what is our reasoning for eating ice cream right now? We conveniently skip asking ourselves "Why?" and connect the dots . . . because we have a habit of making this mistake, and bad decision makers never break this habit and important goals remain unachieved.

The Good: A Valid "Why"

HOW IT SHOULD WORK:

1. A decision presents itself.
2. Clarify the options (your possible actions).
3. For each option, which possible action comes closest to achieving a goal you have set for yourself, if any?
4. If the chosen action gets you closer to your goal, it is *good*!

The Bad: The Why Doesn't Bridge the Gap

Every day we have options and decisions that we could do . . . but we don't do them. Why? For example, you *could* fly to Paris next month. Why aren't you? Answer: A trip to Paris isn't in your success path to accomplish an important goal. If it were, Your Action = Trip to Paris! We are always focused upon what we want, especially what we want right now. However, it's the stuff we want in the future that is hard to connect right now. For instance, the college student wants to be recruited to a top company in the future. Right now, he has the choice to study hard or drink beer. The beer is looking tasty and that career thing is way down the road. He has a decision to make. How does he help himself?

We help ourselves by connecting our actions to our goals with a why. The action is justified because the why can bridge to future success. In the case where our action does not clearly contribute to our goal, we have an "invalid why" because it doesn't provide support for the goal. If we go ahead and choose this action with an invalid why, it is a bad move. We cannot get the time, the money, or the effort back. In fact, we will never know what we missed—which is sometimes the real tragedy of choosing poorly. For example, if your goal for family includes a spouse with children, what are you doing wasting time with this non-matrimonial material you've found? Wouldn't it be a tragedy if you missed the ultimate introduction to your soul mate because you chose to continue dating this person with your "invalid why"?

The consequences from invalid whys are completely unknown and will only be revealed later when you may find you are swimming with the sharks.

Naturally Wrong, Part 2—Becoming "The Decisionator"

As mentioned above, there are two ways we fail at decision making. Part One dealt with being reasonably sure that what we are about to choose is justified (our why) in light of our success objective. The tricky thing about Part One: It assumes we have a clear mind and are able to think reasonably. However, this is often not the case. Nope, we place ourselves (and our minds) at a decision disadvantage every day because other forces are contaminating our thinking. Therefore, the second type of decision-making error occurs when we make decisions with an altered mind. ***Please introduce yourself to The Decisionator. He is you at your worst.***

The "Decisionator" Can Destroy Us All

I've seen him: the arch villain inserting himself into my story, interfering with the happy ending by messing with my mind. He is The Decisionator. He is not welcome when I am trying to figure out what to do. He is me at my worst.

In my Jekyll and Hyde moments, I am The Decisionator. In this state, I can ruin a good decision with little effort. I am not of a balanced or reasonable mind. In this mode, the deck is stacked against my best interests. In this condition, I am not fit to make a good decision; my odds are horrible. In fact, if I make a good decision while also The Decisionator, it was pure coincidence.

Traits of The Decisionator

"Know thyself," said the great Greek philosopher Socrates (469–399 BC). His argument was that we must "know thyself" in order to be wise. Part of decision-making wisdom is knowing when we are less than capable of making a decision. For an adult, it's like knowing when you have consumed too much alcohol. Recognize it and then be careful. We are able to, on almost an hourly basis, turn into The Decisionator. How and why this happens, once you know yourself, is valuable to know. The goal henceforth will be to recognize when The Decisionator has taken the stage and realize how your next decision can be negatively affected.

So, what are the factors that turn us into poor decision makers? Wouldn't it be helpful to recognize these easily? One thing these all have in common is that they are all factors of right now, only applying to this moment. With effort, many of them can be resolved.

DESPERATION

We are desperate when we feel like we don't have options at the moment. We could be short on money, time, energy, or any necessary solution. Desperation does nothing to assist decision making—it only hurts your process. Desperate circumstances are separate from the decision itself. From previous chapters, we have learned that defining success is critically important so we can choose a course that reasonably moves us closer to success. So, in a desperate condition, success may be defined in short terms.

"I'm out of money."

"Success would be paying rent this month."

"Does this option get me closer to paying rent more than any other option?"

Thus, The Decisionator feeds on desperation. Starve him by separating circumstances from the facts about your options.

HURRIED

"Haste makes waste."

—BENJAMIN FRANKLIN

Nothing meaningful needs to be decided quickly unless your life is in danger. When we are asked to hurry up and decide something, we each handle that pressure differently. If I told you to hurry up on stage and give an impromptu speech, you may be fine, or likely not! Speed is a bad thing when the urgency is coming from anyone or anything but you. Thus, being hurried enables The Decisionator to emerge, and "but I had to decide quickly" becomes an excuse for a bad result. Looking at it another way, the time saved rushing a decision will likely be used instead dealing with regret.

Stop and ask yourself, "What's the hurry?" Fast deals are never the best deals. Your sense of urgency is created by you and/or a great salesperson. Don't listen to either. Rarely is an opportunity lost in a matter of minutes. Perhaps 0.001 percent of the time are you offered a choice so amazing, but it must be chosen instantly. A good, lasting career, partnership, marriage, company, vacation, experience never happens in a hurry.

"The car salesman says the sale ends today—so I've got to decide."

"Success would be buying the best car at the best price."

"Is this the only car in this condition? I need to find more like it. If I offered them the sale price tomorrow, they would not refuse my money. I am not going to rush because they say so."

The secret to conquering this Decisionator factor is to never let time paint you in a corner. If you find yourself pinched by the need to hurry, your available options may seem few, but don't play The Decisionator's game. Tell anyone involved that you are considering your options.

PRIDE

"Through pride we are ever deceiving ourselves.
But deep down below the surface of the average conscience,
a still, small voice says to us, something is out of tune."

—C. G. JUNG

Pride is an inwardly directed emotion that carries two common meanings. With a negative connotation, pride refers to an inflated sense of one's personal status or accomplishments. With a positive connotation, pride refers to a satisfied sense of attachment toward one's own or another's choices and actions, or toward a whole group of people, and is a product of praise, independent self-reflection, or a fulfilled feeling of belonging. The Decisionator works with the negative form of pride—an inflated sense of self.

As I have learned more about myself through the years, I absolutely dislike the impact pride has had on my experiences and my results. This Decisionator factor is absolutely this author's Achilles heel. Why is this? The answer I've come up with is that my pride (even false pride) is a source of strength (appropriate or not) and I utilize it at my most challenging entrepreneur moments. Pride is sometimes all we have in our worst moments. But, I realized only recently, pride is not a tool that I can use. Psychologically, ***pride is a balancing factor between our internal value and the external world—but it is nearly worthless in decision making.*** How could it be worthless? We cannot measure pride nor cash it in. It stiffens our spine and creates poorly designed ultimatums. Pride is a barrier to humility (yes, I could be wrong!) and negotiations. Pride has nothing to do with our options. The phrase "swallowing our pride" is appropriate now and again for every self-aware human.

Thus, The Decisionator thrives upon a prideful mind because what is in play is emotion and not the hard currency of facts seen through objective eyes. The trick to defeating The Decisionator is to privately identify that you are in a prideful condition, for whatever reason, and begin writing down the facts that both you and an objective person would agree upon. Essentially, you are not writing down the emotion that is clouding your mind and you will make a better decision.

EGO

Ego, running alongside pride, is our feeling of worth and appearance as compared to/viewed by others. Are we winning or losing? Looking good or looking bad? Picture yourself at the top of the high diving board at your childhood pool. Suddenly your ego is incredibly aware of the people staring at you and overtakes your other instincts for the task at hand or your personal safety. You crash-land a belly flop. Ouch. Why does it hurt when our ego is bruised? Enter The Decisionator, who will joyfully help us do whatever it takes to fill up our ego ASAP—regardless of how much it degrades our decisions.

So what is affecting our ego? Should we add one to the public loss column? Your ego will be bruised for several reasons: (1) right now you might feel like you aren't as good as you thought you were; (2) you misjudged something or someone; (3) you are associated with a failure; (4) you have nothing to show for your time or money.

The Decisionator feeds on embarrassment, self-doubt, and our feeling like a victim. Bruised egos cause us to search for immediate repairs—regardless of the long-term costs. People go shopping, start a rebound relationship, sell things hastily—essentially making bad deals immediately feel better. We also can do damage with a bruised ego. We say things we would never otherwise say, slam doors that are best left open, and test relationships that shouldn't have been tested.

The best method toward clear decision making involves excusing The Decisionator's participation by recognizing your bruised ego and telling yourself, "I've got this." Remind yourself that no matter how bruised your ego becomes, if you acted with integrity, you will not be defined by any possible setback. Move on with the objective facts, decide, and get to the first milestone on the road to success. An immediate remedy is to reach out to people who love and support you.

ANGER

"Angry people are not always wise."

—JANE AUSTEN, *PRIDE AND PREJUDICE*

Everyone gets angry, and this decision-killing factor is easier to understand than most. Very simply, "blinded by anger" is a real condition, and in that state, we cannot think clearly. Anger invites The Decisionator to take over. It is a reaction to damaged pride and bruised egos. It is human. We get frustrated, disappointed, betrayed, and lied to—it's part of dealing with people. We can even be angry with ourselves. What is certain is that anger is temporary. We must pause, recognize that we are angry, let it subside, and let our minds and instincts work clearly through what must be decided. The Decisionator can be quickly defeated with a pause in this case. As a timely example, if President Donald J. Trump could master this control, he could be twice as effective with his message—avoiding a majority of communication errors.

FEAR/GRIEF

> *"No one ever told me that grief felt so like fear. I am not afraid, but the sensation is like being afraid. At other times it feels like being mildly drunk, or concussed. There is a sort of invisible blanket between the world and me."*
>
> —C. S. LEWIS

Fear for the future and/or grief over the future without someone we love leaves us looking for emotional safety. We can be short-sighted and impetuous in our decision making, as we just want to feel better. For example, a frequent fraud victim is the widow who must make decisions without her husband. Separating feelings of fear or grief from the decision is the only way to think clearly and avoid being The Decisionator.

REJECTION

"A boo is a lot louder than a cheer."

—LANCE ARMSTRONG

Rejection is an instance that immediately impacts pride and ego, discussed above. I specifically want to highlight the incredible power of rejection to invite The Decisionator to take over. We have our ideas rejected. We are socially rejected because we aren't invited to join the group. We are emotionally rejected by another. Sometimes a school, client, career, or company will reject us. What is hurt by rejection? In this case, I care about how rejection affects your next decision. Rejection makes us emotional and unwanted, walking away. It's a low point. Multiple rejections (multiple lows) in a row are excruciatingly tough to experience. So what do we do?

You know the difference between good and bad decision makers. You know the pitfalls of decisions made without defined success. Finally, you know that The Decisionator affects every human being. So, now that you know these things, recognize that if you are rejected, it's not you. The rejection happens due to the decision-making discipline used by the other party. They could be completely flawed—but it's their process . . . and you have yours. Your decision-making process is likely better than theirs at this moment. So, get moving toward someone or something that wants you as much as you want them, and don't give rejection as much power over your perspective as you have in the past.

FATIGUE

"The formula was simple: E + F + C = M.
That is, excitement plus fatigue, plus confusion equals mistakes."
—RUTLEDGE ETHERIDGE, *AGENT OF DESTRUCTION*

When we are fatigued, we are vulnerable in many ways. Without a fresh reserve of vitality, we are less optimistic (even pessimistic) and we will judge things too harshly (e.g., "I'm so tired of this")—which alters perspective. We are also vulnerable because the mind doesn't have the reserve energy—which lowers thinking power. Enter The Decisionator . . . to just "get it over with." If we don't recognize that we are fatigued, we will have to live with less than desirable results as The Decisionator. The answer here is similar to anger: Have the discipline to recognize your condition and force a pause to recover and rejuvenate. Phrases such as "sleep on it" or "things will look better tomorrow" are about pausing to let your body catch up with your opportunity. In a baseball analogy, don't step to the plate with a foggy mind or a cracked bat. Recognize that you should return to the dugout and retool before taking your swing. If you can do this, The Decisionator cannot get into the game.

HOPE/OPTIMISM

"I don't like hope very much. In fact, I hate it. It's the crystal meth of emotions. It hooks you fast and kills you hard. It's bad news. The worst. It's sharp sticks and cherry bombs. When hope shows up, it's only a matter of time until someone gets hurt."

—JENNIFER DONNELLY, *REVOLUTION*

How can hope and optimism be bad in our decision making? This is one of the most difficult traits to detect because we are naturally hopeful creatures. Using hope, we build bridges across great gaps in our realities. Hope and optimism are fine as a way to greet the world. However, they should not be used in decisions. They taint reality.

He says: "Honey, will you marry me?"
She replies: "But you are an alcoholic. I cannot marry that."
He says: "I'll quit drinking."
<She builds a hope bridge at this moment>
She says: "Then I will marry you."

I am amazed at how many times I have failed and seen my close friends fail due to hope bridging the decision-making process. For instance, visualize that you are buying a used car that seems to be a good one. You circle the car, looking it over, looking under, driving it briefly, etc. Why do we not drive a car one hundred miles and take it to a certified mechanic before buying? What shortens our critical thinking as we look for the negatives in something (or someone) is that we substitute further digging with hope and new belief that things will work out well. We're so anxious to move forward that we carelessly slide hope into the driver's seat.

"In the factory, we make cosmetics. In the drug store, we sell hope."

—REVLON FOUNDER, CHARLES REUSON

For a more damaging example, several middle-aged, single friends of mine found someone online who seemed like a great match. Within a year of two weddings and one engagement, unfortunate reality was discovered by each person who failed to think critically and relied upon hope instead. These incredible people my friends each found were no longer incredible! In fact, they were a heartbreaking disappointment with incredible baggage that was never explored well enough. These are bright people. Where did they go wrong?

What happens to critical thinking when we want something to work out so much? Part denial, part hope, and part throwing-ourselves-to-the-wind, our decision making gets progressively worse. ***Hope is bad for decisions.***

DEPRESSION

Everyone gets depressed at one time or another. The most insidious factor enabling The Decisionator's ability to hurt our decision making is depression. I am not a doctor, but I have been depressed during times of chronic extended stress, and I decided to find out why. You can ask your doctor and search the Internet for more information, but I believe it's important for you to clearly understand today how brain chemicals can affect decision making.

Neurotransmitters are the brain chemicals that communicate information throughout our brain and body. They relay signals between nerve cells, called "neurons." The brain uses neurotransmitters to tell your heart to beat, your lungs to breathe, and your stomach to digest. They can also affect mood, sleep, concentration, and weight, and can cause adverse symptoms when they are out of balance. Neurotransmitter levels can be depleted in many ways. As a matter of fact, it is estimated that eighty-six percent of Americans have suboptimal neurotransmitter levels.

There are three key "balance" brain neurotransmitters that work in concert to significantly impact how we feel and how we react to people and decisions: dopamine, serotonin, and norepinephrine. We are always naturally producing these chemicals for our brain to use. These chemicals are the target of nearly all antidepressive medications, with the goal of elevating these chemicals to normal levels. However, some people are naturally low on these chemicals and, more commonly, we humans do things to alter these chemical levels. Certain factors bring down the levels of these chemicals: chronic stress, anxiety, illness, genetics, lack of sleep, lack of exercise, neurotoxins, poor diet, drug/alcohol abuse. I believe any human working hard to get somewhere comes up against these factors at one time or another and experiences a depression of these essential brain neurotransmitters. These are the low moments.

For more detail on these three chemicals and the decision-making impact they bring, you can read the Digging Deeper section. I want to emphasize that The Decisionator often takes the stage when these chemicals are depressed. Clinical depression is not just about attitude, perspective, or wanting things to be different. It is a chemical imbalance issue, too. You either have enough of a chemical or you don't. If you're low, you are absorbing more than you are producing—and that is where the problem begins for a clear decision.

Digging Deeper . . .

Dopamine is our main focus neurotransmitter. When dopamine is either elevated or low, we can have focus issues such as not remembering where we put our keys, forgetting what a paragraph said when we just finished reading it, or simply daydreaming and not being able to stay on task. Dopamine is also responsible for our drive or desire to get things done—or motivation.[4] Dopamine stimulates happiness and excitability and can improve your overall contentedness. Dopamine is the chemical in the brain triggered by several drugs, including caffeine, cocaine, and alcohol, to create the sensation of happiness. Essentially, we eat, drink, and ingest chemicals, as urges, to spike our dopamine levels. When dopamine is low, we will self-medicate by doing or ingesting whatever makes us feel better, chemically. So, late-night ice cream is more than ice cream! Our brains are crafty in knowing what we can do to raise dopamine, oftentimes in a way that is harmful in the long term.

....

4 "What are Neurotransmitters?" Neurogistics, accessed November 30, 2016, http://www.neurogistics.com/the-science/what-are-neurotransmitters.

For decision making, low dopamine makes us vulnerable to choosing what feels good over what is good for our success plan. Low dopamine trumps all "whys" until it is satisfied. Thus, a success definition of "fit and trim and healthy" will have a low probability when we are self-medicating with food, drink, and behavior that brings the opposite in the short term. If you examine your impulsive behavior like I have, a majority of it is simply satisfying a dopamine fix for the moment. To make good decisions, dopamine levels cannot be wanting.

Serotonin, affectionately called the "feel good" neurotransmitter, provides an overall feeling of well-being. Adequate amounts of serotonin are necessary for a stable mood and the ability to remain calm. Serotonin levels can affect how we view, give, and receive love and intimacy. Caffeine can cause a depletion of serotonin over time. Serotonin also regulates many other processes such as carbohydrate cravings, sleep cycle, pain control, appropriate digestion, and immune system function.

For decision making, low serotonin levels make us vulnerable to being The Decisionator! Serotonin greatly affects how we react to all of the above: being angry, hurried, or rejected, hits to our pride, or bruises to our ego. Serotonin is significant in our sleep quality, and that impacts our fatigue levels. So, low serotonin greatly enables The Decisionator. What a discovery! Normal serotonin levels are a good decision's foundation.

Norepinephrine affects parts of the brain where attention and responses are controlled. Norepinephrine affects heart rate, triggers the release of glucose from energy stores, and increases blood flow to skeletal muscle. It increases the brain's oxygen supply. A sudden, rapid rise of norepinephrine causes panic attacks. A somewhat high level makes you happy, and a really high level makes you euphoric. Since norepinephrine plays a role in regulating our hunger and

Continued

eating responses, individuals with low norepinephrine may experience greater levels of hunger and appetite—and weight gain.

For decision making, norepinephrine affects us in many ways. Low levels of norepinephrine bog us down, leaving us with a significant reduction in both energy and motivation, resulting in a depressed, take-no-action feeling that doesn't go away. So, low norepinephrine tends to make doing nothing the default choice among our options. We are mindful of our success goals yet we don't have the means to get up and get going. We are The Decisionator when we fail to act. Thus, we can slam the door on The Decisionator when we recognize low norepinephrine and deal with it.

THE GOOD NEWS

The above three neurotransmitter levels in our brain can be raised naturally. If that doesn't work, our doctor can help with one or all of them. It's only chemistry. Most important to keep in mind: We are trying to put our brain in the *best* position to make a decision, and we cannot leave the back door open for The Decisionator to sneak in and screw up our results.

Naturally Wrong, Part 3—Ignoring the Consequences

Sometimes we don't know if we have a valid why—we just want to enjoy life without thinking too hard. Even with a clear mind (not The Decisionator), we still can't be sure whether we should choose option A or B. In these times, we must consider the possible consequences of all options. It is an easy exercise: "If I do A, the possible consequences are __________. If I do B, the consequences are __________." "If I do nothing, the consequences are __________." Our parents told us about consequences while growing up, of course. Why were we told to not take candy from strangers, play in the street, hang out with the wrong people, stay out too late, spend money we didn't have? It is/was the consequences they were thinking about on our behalf.

For fun, you can use a simple test to see how you tend to consider consequences today. As a driver, how low do you let the fuel gauge dip toward empty before filling up? "How low do you go?" For me, I know I can take the fuel level down to the last ten miles, and I do that often. The consequences of being late and calling AAA are acceptable to me. On the other hand, my wife gets nervous under one-fourth tank of gas and her car is usually fueled up. For her, the consequences *feel* more significant than for me. Which type are you? It's a personal judgment about tolerance, and neither is wrong; it's just how we are built. If you are sensitive to consequences, you must make choices that will only produce possible consequences you can tolerate.

Consequences of our decisions really matter! Becoming an expert on calculating the possible consequences of any choice can keep you on track for the life you want. These ever-important consequences come in a few types. Let's dig deeper to make better decisions with common sense.

MILD: Consequences That Stop/Slow Progress

The least damaging consequences are those that only slow us down or stop us temporarily—like walking in deep snow. They create a pause but do not take us off our expected progress track. Consequences that stop/slow progress can require saying, "I'm sorry," trying again, getting assistance, regrouping, redoing, or reselling. We can fix it and move on—like changing a flat tire and continuing on our road trip. We can still achieve the goal in mind because we were just paused briefly.

MEDIUM: Consequences That Require Cleanup

Have you ever carried so many dishes or glasses to/from the dining table that others were alarmed? "I've got it!" you say confidently. However, you internally decide that you are OK with the possible cleanup consequences. If you drop these breakable items, a mop and broom can tidy up in fifteen minutes. More significant are the consequences that require us to stop and dedicate additional effort to cleaning up a mess in our lives. Unintended cleanups can derail our locomotive off the train track of life. Consequences that require cleanup can include quitting anything, breaking up, dissolving a partnership, financial losses, moving, reputation repair, lost trust, lost love, and hurting your loved ones. I rarely make a decision that could bring significant cleanup consequences because big cleanup efforts can kill all my momentum for an unknown amount of time. However, some cleanups are a natural part of moving on and involve healing and readjustment. In those cases, we move into those consequences intentionally and purposely as part of a decision to take the pain and move forward in our life.

SEVERE: Consequences That Are Permanent

Alternatively, the most damaging consequences are those that force change upon us and remove options and flexibility from our future. These are not always horrible and can sometimes have beautiful stories that include overcoming adversity—but they definitely force us down a path we would not have chosen first. Permanent consequence examples can include early pregnancy, bankruptcy, disability, criminal conviction, overdose, accidents, injuries, and breaking someone's heart.

I've seen people make poor choices on big decisions in their twenties and thirties, and they are dealing with the permanent consequences of those decisions their whole lives. Their potential was cut short and they had to adjust their dreams downward due to permanent consequences. They talk about their regrets in terms of permanent consequences. They think about, "What if?"

Deciding with Consequences in Mind: "Can I Handle It?"

So, when I am making decisions and I am not sure about the proper choice—even after considering why and all the options with a clear mind—I think about the consequences. The question to ask is "If the decision turns out badly, can I accept the possible consequences?" How much risk can I handle? In terms of consequences, what is my exposure in this decision? Sometimes, the possible consequences of a potential choice are too large to handle. For me, I don't do things that have consequences I could not personally stand. I would kick myself forever. In the cost/benefit analysis of consequences at a fork in the road, a choice is a loser when it has more potential costs than potential benefits, especially when the consequences are severe and permanent.

LET'S LOOK AT SOME LIFE EXAMPLES

- Asking a romantic interest for a date: Is a possible rejection worth a possible "yes"? Of course. Romantics must be brave to make the world go 'round.
- Running across the street while dodging traffic: Is the benefit worth the potential cost? Obviously not. We call these actions foolish.
- Quitting a job and starting a business: If the business fails, can I get another job? Can my family survive the possible disruption? If so, then what is stopping you?
- Buying a home or auto at the top end of our price range: If I cannot make the payments at any point, am I OK with losing it?
- Staying partnered with someone who has hurt you: If things do not improve, can I leave at any time? Can I accept being hurt again?

- Having unprotected sex: Am I ready to start a family? Am I prepared to make a life/death decision for an unborn child? Am I willing to catch an STD?
- Not doing something when I had the chance: Will I regret forever not trying? How painful will it be to kick myself because I didn't at least try?

Large Consequence Juggling

I have never been able to function well while juggling multiple large consequence risks and I don't advise anyone to do so. This means that you have made more than one decision that could go bad and deliver large consequences. If two or three of these break down at the same time, we can be sucked into a tornado of regret and cleanup work. It can ruin us. Chronic gamblers and people with addictions do this frequently because their disease overwhelms their ability to correctly evaluate consequences. I don't advise "going for broke" because, while the rewards could be great, we can live without that possibility. On the other hand, we cannot always live well with multiple bad decision consequences crashing to earth.

Another Cost of Consequence Juggling: Chronic Stress

When we have one potential consequence mess, we can watch it, be prepared for it, and, if it happens, deal with it capably. However, if we have more than one, our instincts kick in and our natural anxiety level goes way up—adding chronic

Continued

stress to our body that doesn't go away until the threat is over. Chronic stress damages our health and puts a lot of pressure on us that we cannot control.

I have lived with this in business and it feels ugly. In my situation years ago, a struggling business combined with an active lawsuit and the needs of my young family created my resolve to write this chapter! Multiple active large possible negative consequences create an instinctive threat condition. The threat is there when you are awake and it's there during your sleep. We cannot deny our instincts, as they are there to protect us. When instincts are triggering anxiety over possible bad outcomes, they are telling us to find a way to stop juggling more than one possible bad consequence at a time—clawing our way to something that is manageable.

As my parental instincts tell me to not let my child play in the middle of the street, there are limits to what consequences I am willing to accept if they should happen. As a husband and father, I will take risks that can impact me but I will not take risks that could severely impact people I love. However, I take business risks every year that could significantly alter our standard of living. But I won't lead my closest family members and friends into a crash by juggling multiple possible consequences. I can tolerate losing money, but I will not tolerate having to start over. The consideration of consequences in this way keeps me from being stupid and hurting others (and myself). Thus, I don't gamble with more than fun money, I don't risk my health, I don't carry debt I cannot repay, and I work in whatever manner it takes to make enough money to meet the needs of today and the near future. There will always be college loans, car wreck deductibles, kids' braces, medical bills, and you name it—many other needs. I won't risk being unable to do what is necessary. Therefore, when I make my decisions and I am considering consequences, the consequences I cannot accept will remove those choices as options for me. Sometimes, that removes all the options and there is no decision to make!

Using Consequences as a Shortcut

When the correct choice is not clear due to our why (a lack of an overriding goal that supports the option), we can use consequences as a shortcut to the right answer. When you think about the possible consequences for each option you could choose, figure out the consequence category you are possibly choosing: *progress-slowing* (mild) vs. *cleanup* (medium) vs. *permanent* (severe) consequences. The category should tell you how much thought this decision deserves. Choosing the option with the most acceptable consequences is the best action until you define a goal in this area. Pausing to at least consider consequences and their severity will prevent most extraordinarily stupid decisions, in my experience.

Breaking the "Bad Decision" Addiction

When presented with a decision, a fork in the road, an opportunity you can take/not take, something you can pursue or leave behind, perform this three-step review:

1. "Do I have a valid why in the choice I am about to make?"
2. "Is my mind thinking clearly (or am I The Decisionator)?"
3. "Are the consequences of failure acceptable?"

The answer to Question #1 (Why?) is hopefully yes, as you can link the choice you are making to a goal. If so, great. That's big support for this choice. If you aren't sure, the next two questions are even more important. Question #2 needs you to be honest about your state of mind as you make the decision. Is your mind clear and unaffected by the traits of The Decisionator? If not, you must neutralize why you are The Decisionator before making a clear-headed decision. Finally, for the option you prefer, Question #3 needs to know if you are aware of the possible consequences and can accept them. The goal is yes—yes—yes in this series of questions. We have honored our objectives, cleared our mind, and examined the hard facts in order to decide.

Can you see your decision-making tools starting to come together? I assure you that you are already thinking differently about decisions. Now that we know how and why we make poor decisions, we are that much more empowered to deal with the feelings and ramifications of a bad decision, which we will discuss in the next chapters. What happens when we choose poorly?

·7·

DECISIONS CAUSE US PAIN

When we are right, we seldom give our decision much thought because we expected to be right. A quick pat on the back and we move forward in what is (hopefully) a streak of good decisions. We have momentum and we are moving faster because of good results. However, when we are unsure of our decision-making ability, we create natural pain for ourselves that is in addition to the consequences of any decision failure.

Types of Decision-Making Pain

Within decision-making efforts, we experience three types of pain: anxiety, regret, and consequences. There is a suspense and penance we carry for every decision, sometimes for hours and sometimes for a lifetime. This pain can be illustrated as shown:

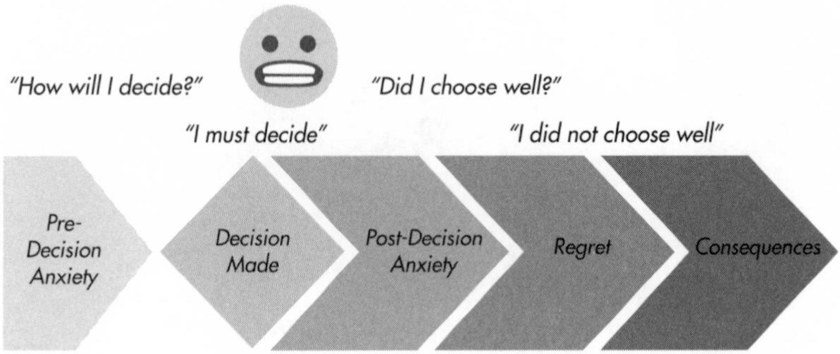

Anxiety

Everyone is afraid of choosing poorly. We have anxiety before and after a decision. Some people are paralyzed in front of a decision, where simply buying a car or signing a lease or committing emotionally strikes great fear into their hearts. Decision anxiety is heightened by the fear of being wrong. Anxiety over decisions affects our sense of peace and can physically alter how our bodies function. Anxiety can make us sick.

Pre-decision anxiety is amplified by whether or not we have confidence in our decision-making discipline. If we are confident we have a process that works, we are able to trump the anxiety and put ourselves in the position to shine. If we are not confident and have no sure process, our anxiety grows greater until time is up and we must choose. This can be painful, and there is certainly a cost to anxiety.

We can credit our instincts for the growing anxiety around a big decision. Our internal sense of survival is well tested by our ancestors to lean toward what is best for us. When our mind knows we are only performing the trial-and-error method of decision making, it instinctively knows that we are possibly in a worse position and panic is justified. So, to suppress anxiety is to deaden a good warning signal. Alternatively, when we "notice" our anxiety, we are best served to remind ourselves that a decision is at our feet and it's time to do what we have learned about decision making.

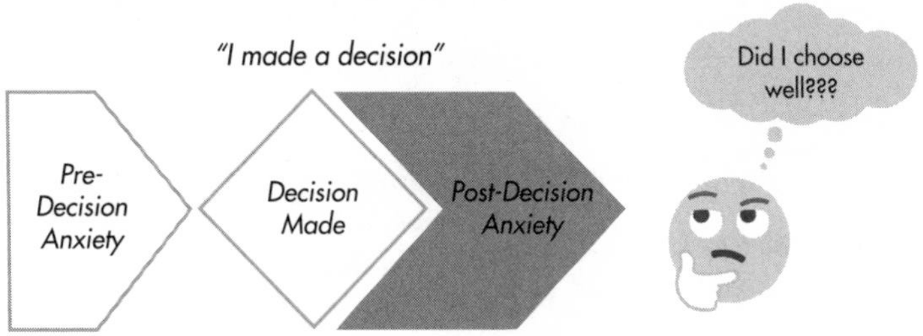

Post-decision anxiety is the highest when we use the trial-and-error method, and anxiety is lowest when we have connected our *action* to our *goal* with a valid why. Of course we all hope we made the right decision. We can be confident, too, if we used our decision-making discipline, and confidence always lowers post-decision anxiety. For example, if you bought a new car and it's the only car you took for a test-drive, you will have higher post-purchase anxiety than someone who test-drove six cars and knows they chose the best car of the six. The same can be said for dating and marriage. If you only date the one person you marry, you will likely be more anxious post-marriage than the person who dated many and knows that this person was the best of the lot.

Regret

"Anxiety over a bad decision turns to regret when you have confirmation."

The first time I thought of this statement, I laughed out loud with relief because I had been pondering the *source* of regret. I had been asking myself, "Where does regret come from?" I have since realized that regret is not created. Rather, it is converted. Anxiety of the past is turned into regret in the present once the missing ingredient is added: confirmation of failure. Our anxiety (the failure we imagined possible) was hypothetical until we finally found solid confirmation.

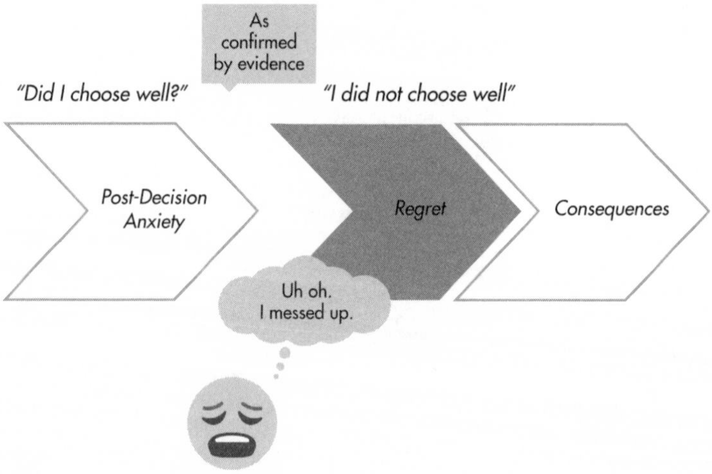

Here are some common regrets that were anxieties until confirmed:

REGRETS IN THE SHORT TERM

- "I should have ordered what you ordered"—My wife often tells me this after she tastes what I ordered and confirms for herself that it is fantastic.
- "I knew I should have gone with you"—When I confirm that my errands included something my kids like but they declined my invitation.
- "I should have gone to that concert"—What I tell myself when I have declined to go see a band I love and a friend confirms for me, "It was the greatest!"

REGRETS IN THE LONG TERM

- "I should never have broken up with him/her"—Confirmed when you see the person later, successful, happy, and on the arm of someone else . . . And, in hindsight, of greater interest than the one you chose. It's an exhilarating and sad confirmation that carries lifelong regret.
- "I should have followed my passion"—Confirmed when you realize that money is not as valuable as originally thought or when the years shorten to eliminate the "someday" fantasy you tell yourself.
- "I knew I couldn't trust him/her"—Confirmed by something the other person could no longer hide.

- "I should have never made that deal"—Confirmed when the deal goes south, the money or time is gone, and you have nothing to show for it but a lesson.
- "I should never have sold that car"—Confirmed every time you see one like it on the road and you know it was a classic that brought you special joy.
- "I should have traveled when I had the opportunity"—Confirmed when the person who went in your place appears to have done fabulously, or, confirmed when the likelihood of you traveling there is becoming less and less.

THE GHOST (AND COST) OF REGRET

The cost of regret is the continual revisiting of "what we should have done" whenever something reminds us of an old decision. It's like a lifetime penance we pay, a decision jail sentence we serve for a while or the rest of our lives. There is an incredible cost to regret because each time we experience regret, our immediate momentum is paused, a negative vibe body-slams our psyche, and we have to swallow a hit to our confidence. Regret simply sucks.

Regret . . . our mind will not let go of it. Why is that?

Our mind awakens the ghost of regret for one simple reason: The original decision had at least two forks in the road. Since then, facts have confirmed that one of the forks was a bad choice. Now the mind can only replay the decision with the fork that was confirmed as good and torment us. And, like a ghost, it lives on and on . . . haunting our present. This ghost is only silenced with confidence that we made the best decision possible at the time we made it.

Consequences: The Ropes That Bind Us

Imagine you are tied tightly with rope—bound so tightly it hurts. The pain you feel is the result of trying to move. Your flexibility and choices are limited when tied. These are **consequences**. It is the same result with bad decisions. Each bad decision is a rope wrapped around us, restricting our movement. They cause us pain and frustration because we cannot do what we want to do.

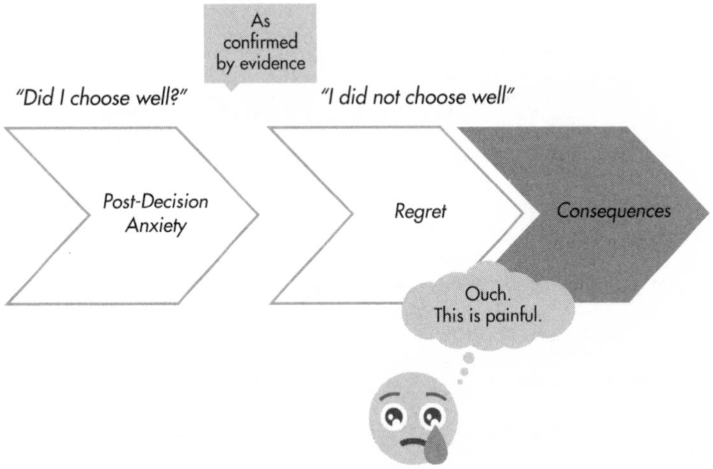

Also, if we are tied up with consequences from our past decisions, we cannot invent, we don't have creative time, we don't have extra money, we are heavily burdened, we are stressed, and we are not free to thrive. Can you feel the ropes? Consequences are painful when we try to move forward.

No Pain Prescription

Decision-making pain is always possible, but it can be minimized. Pre- and post-decision *anxiety* is eliminated by your confidence that you are following good decision-making discipline. If we made the best decision possible at the time, we cannot second-guess ourselves nearly as much, and that leaves little room for *regret* in the future. Also, we can prevent bad *consequences* by a series of good decisions so we are not tied down by the ropes that can bind us.

Now, let's examine how bad decisions happen. What really goes on behind the scenes? It's not a simple matter!

PERSONAL EXERCISE:
Regret Inventory

We humans wander the earth loaded with regrets. Yet what is the value of doing so? Regret only has value if we can use it to make better decisions going forward. Let's use it now for that purpose.

For each question below, please make a handwritten response. Perhaps use a separate sheet of paper to record your thoughts that come to mind for each category.

1. **Money**: My biggest regret(s) about money are:
2. **Romantic Relationships**: My biggest regret(s) about my romantic relationship(s) are:

3. **Education**: My biggest regret(s) about my current education level are:
4. **Career**: My biggest regret(s) about my current career are:
5. **Opportunities**: My biggest regret(s) about opportunities I should have taken are:
6. **Health**: My biggest regret(s) about my current health are:
7. **Purchases**: My biggest regret(s) about things I have purchased are:
8. **Friendships**: My biggest regret(s) about my friendships are:
9. **Legal**: My biggest regret(s) about legal matters are:
10. **Family**: My biggest regret(s) about my parents, siblings, or children are:
11. **Future Setup**: My biggest regret(s) about how prepared and ready I am for my desired future are:

This is the low point of this book, I promise. How do you feel? For some of us, rethinking these thoughts can be tough. Just remember, we cannot change the past, and we are using the past to create a better tomorrow.

If you have many regrets, it is confirmation that better decision making is needed and will create dividends. Regret is a natural human condition, and it tells us something about what we value. Regretting something means you care about it.

Let's take a deep breath now . . . and also remember that this is a journey of self-discovery. The improvement path involves learning, thinking, feeling, and acting. You will feel better as we get closer to actions that will make a difference in your future. It is our feelings right now that serve as motivation to make real change.

A Movie Climax of Regret

One of my favorite movie illustrations of regret, demonstrated by brilliant actors Clint Eastwood and Meryl Streep, is *The Bridges of Madison County*. The climax of the movie involves Meryl's character deciding whether to stay with her old life or start a new life with Clint's character. It is exhilarating, hopeful, and sad—all at once—because the viewer knows that whatever choice she makes, she will regret the alternative choice forever. The viewer is in the position of trying to decide for her which choice will have the greatest benefit and least regret. The movie takes the viewer on a journey of possible regret.

So, imagine you are now waving good-bye to these old regrets. You've listed them. We've repurposed them for fuel on our journey forward. But we don't need them hanging around in our rear-view mirror.

"Good-bye, regrets. I am no longer going to visit you. I am starting a new chapter where I am in more control. I know what I want, and I intend to create a lot of decision dividends for myself."

·8·

WE CAN DO BETTER

Let's take the focus off of you for a moment and look at someone else. *How much poor decision making can people do and still be successful?* Think about some famous successful people: Steve Jobs (stubborn to change his mind), Thomas Edison (vengeful to competitors), Benjamin Franklin (an internal perfectionist), Margaret Thatcher (arrogance in accomplishments), President Donald Trump (arrogance in self-worth), and even President Bill Clinton (playboy). Successful people like these usually have one fatal flaw that creates poor decision making, but they rarely have more than one. They may have bad marriages, they may be arrogant, and they may have small regrets, but, they almost never make bad decisions in more than one area of their life on their way to achieving great things.

Only one? Why am I certain of this point, you may ask? The answer is simple. Poor decisions combine for a multiplier effect. They don't just add up—they multiply to create conditions that do not help you reach your goals. We cannot afford more than *one* bad category of decisions *at the same time* in our lifetime. Much like your car, you can handle one flat tire because you have a spare tire—and you are back on the road in an hour or less. However, you cannot deal with two or more flat tires at the same time, as you will be off the road or wrecked for some time and certainly late to the party. The costs are unknowable but significant. Look at the people you consider successful and ponder their decision making. I bet you will find one or fewer poor decision-making categories. If they're famous, *TMZ* or the *National Enquirer* likely has already found it. The good news is that we average Joes don't have to be perfect because everyone has a decision-making flaw, but successful people tend to have only one. So, we must work toward reducing our decision-making flaws, not achieving perfection in decision making.

More about President Bill Clinton

The forty-second president of the United States is fascinating from a decision-making standpoint. Bill arose out of small-town Arkansas in the '70s and '80s to become the most popular president in a long time. Yet he was his own worst enemy where tabloid gossip and women were concerned. Even in the White House, impeachment didn't sink him. Why?

From early in President Clinton's life, he made amazing decisions about who he should know, and the connections to make and loyalties to build. He made a strategic decision to marry Hillary Rodham, as she was the breadwinner for much of his early career. Even in defeat as Arkansas governor for a second term, he made great decisions toward taking back the governorship that would lead to his credentials to be president. He chose the right advisors. All along, he made decisions that put people in the position to help him later and to overcome the problems he created for himself. He always chose the right words to cut the issue. Right or wrong, Bill Clinton was a cunning decision maker in every area of his life but one, and that is why nobody could beat him even when he gave them the stick to do it.

In fact, if we follow the decision-making rules and use the tools in this book, we can be less vulnerable to our biggest flaws that trip us up throughout our lives.

Successful People Aren't Perfect Either

Successful people are successful because they simply achieve the goals they set for their life at the time. The goals do not have to be enormous. Being happy can be the goal. Building the world's tallest building can be the goal. Having zero personal debt can be the goal. Being in the Pro Football Hall of Fame can be the goal. But when we set goals, we begin a series of new decisions and we also inherit all our decisions (and results) from our past.

When we begin to recognize our decisions are getting better in all areas of our life, we begin to receive dividends. At some point the dividends add up. Successful people attain greatness because they work in balance with what I call the "6 Ingredients/Dividends of Good Decision Making" as they direct their lives toward what they want.

The Six Ingredients/Dividends of Good Decision Making

To be able to achieve our goals, we need these things below as *ingredients* so we are in the position to achieve. When we make good decisions, these also come to us as *dividends*:

1. Free time
2. Good health
3. Money
4. Freedom
5. Momentum
6. Joy

Let's briefly discuss each of these to understand how they each serve as an important ingredient in decisions *and* return to us as a dividend. They are not in order of importance.

FREE TIME AS AN INGREDIENT OF GOOD DECISIONS

We can use time to think, invent, plan, reconsider, ask others their opinions, do research, or just recharge. Rushed decisions are usually the bad ones, and time is the prescription for preventing a rushed decision.

FREE TIME AS A DIVIDEND FROM GOOD DECISIONS

Good decisions create more time because we aren't fixing things as often. We don't have to maneuver around our failures—and that saves time. More rest, relaxation, and thinking time make us even more ready for the next challenge.

GOOD HEALTH AS AN INGREDIENT OF GOOD DECISIONS

"I'm not feeling it" I sometimes say as I am invited to go to yoga or attempting to focus upon my writing. This feeling is tied to my health and the communication I am getting from my mind and body. Recalling our discussion in chapter 6, "Traits of The Decisionator," our mental state of mind at the brain chemical level can significantly affect our thinking. We have more options at our disposal when we feel better in mind and body—our health.

"When you have your health, you have everything.
When you do not have your health, nothing else matters at all."

—AUGUSTEN BURROUGHS

GOOD HEALTH AS A DIVIDEND FROM GOOD DECISIONS

As good decisions bring dividends, those benefits include less stress and time for fitness and also relaxation. All of these things contribute to good health, which contributes to the next good decision.

MONEY AS AN INGREDIENT OF GOOD DECISIONS

I've often said that I consider money "fuel" to take me toward my next desired destination. Think about the different mental state we have as we drive our car and the fuel gauge is near empty vs. how good it feels when we know the tank is full. That is the mental state that money (or lack of it) contributes to our decision making. When we have spare cash, we can pursue opportunities, we can quit our job and start something new, we can send her flowers, we can take him to a surprise lunch, we can travel and try new experiences, we can enroll in an interesting class, etc. Decisions made without available money often have little flexibility. It's like getting in your car and deciding where to go, and you look down and the fuel gauge reads empty. How many choices does this driver really have? As in the game Monopoly, I land on a property I want to buy and have no cash—which is a repeated bummer. I can't make any decision because the lack of money has made it for me.

> **I never liked any game of Monopoly I ever played.**
> **I either loved it or hated it: Lesson #1**
> I learned that without spare cash, I was just circling the board, rolling the dice, collecting $200, and avoiding the tax man and bad luck. To me, spare cash determined my options. If I had it, I rolled the dice with more gusto. If I didn't, it was a different game and less fun.

If I smartly purchase a Monopoly property, I can then charge rent—maybe add a motel/hotel and stick it to my opponents—creating dividends for me. In real life, if I acquire more education, I am qualified for the better-paying opportunity. If I choose a good partner, their talent and income combines with mine to create a better standard of living. If my purchasing decisions have been good ones, I have the credit rating to qualify for lower interest rates and bigger loans. In all decisions, money is almost always at stake because we are either going to make more or less money *and* we are going to spend more or less money as the quality of the decision is revealed.

I never liked any game of Monopoly I ever played.
I either loved it or hated it: Lesson #2

The first few rounds of a game of Monopoly set up the destiny of each player. While their landing spots are random, their decisions begin to add up—especially as cash gets tighter. Like the baseball hitter, to choose to not swing (purchase something) is sometimes more valuable. The prestige of owning Park Place is not as worthy as owning cheap motels on Mediterranean Ave. Through the rounds, players begin to see if their collective decisions will make them dividends. In the end, as the name suggests, there can be only one dominant player. That player is almost always the better decision maker, and I never liked watching my friends deliver a twisted smile as we all knew I was not winning that day.

How your partner values and spends money can have an incredible effect upon a business or a marriage. I have friends whose spouses spend more money than they make, creating a "Make More—Spend Even More" scenario. So, (marriage) dividends sometimes take years to be revealed and, unfortunately, they can have been liabilities all along. This is why big decisions make or break us.

Money: Is This Freedom?

In 2015, nearly half of US households—47 percent—say they spend all of their income, go into debt, or dip into savings to meet their annual expenses. If a typical middle-class household had to weather a period of joblessness without any income, they would exhaust their available savings within twenty-one days, the analysis found. If that same family also cashed in all their retirement investments to get by, they would burn through those assets within four months.[5]

MONEY AS A DIVIDEND OF GOOD DECISIONS

"It takes money to make money."

One of my favorite moments involves money coming back to me due to a good decision I made yesterday, last year, or five years ago. Often these are investments I have made in businesses or people or ideas and something has progressed to create money that arrives as a dividend. Sometimes, I invest in improving myself, learning something new, acquiring valuable expertise. When education or training gets you higher paying work, for example, the better income is the dividend. It took money as an ingredient to make progress and the financial dividend is (hopefully) always greater than the original cost. One of my favorite illustrations is when a friend exclaims, "my spouse makes more money than I do!" Their statement is proclaiming that they appreciate the financial dividend

....

5 "The Precarious State of Family Balance Sheets," The Pew Charitable Trusts, January 2015, http://www.pewtrusts.org/~/media/assets/2015/01/fsm_balance_sheet_report.pdf.

that is coming from their decision about whom to marry. It is good discipline to expect that money invested should return a dividend. When the dividend doesn't arrive and plenty of time has elapsed, the outbound money flow should stop.

FREEDOM AS AN INGREDIENT OF GOOD DECISIONS

Time: Is This Freedom?

The percentage of full-time workers in the US has dwindled since the recession began in 2007, but the number of hours they say they work each week has held steady at about forty-seven. While four in ten workers put in a standard forty-hour workweek, many others toil longer than that, including nearly one in five (18%), who work a grueling sixty hours or more. That translates into twelve-hour days from Monday to Friday—or into shorter weekdays with lots of time spent working on the weekends. Salaried workers, on average, work even more, with a full 25% saying they put in at least sixty hours per week. Thus, while workers earning a salary may enjoy greater income than their counterparts who are paid hourly, they do pay a price in lost personal time.[6]

For me, freedom is my overriding objective in life. I want to be free to do what I want to do when I want to do it. Freedom feels

....

6 "The '40-Hour' Workweek Is Actually Longer—by Seven Hours," Lydia Saad, Gallup, August 29, 2014, http://www.gallup.com/poll/175286/hour-workweek-actually-longer-seven-hours.aspx.

good. When someone asks me, "Do you want to go to this?" or, "Check out this opportunity!" if I have the freedom to say "yes" and explore, then I will be able to possibly improve my situation. Freedom is an ingredient of a good decision. However, if I am so constrained that I cannot do things due to lack of freedom, I cannot participate in what's next. It's like being asked to open a door with your hands tied behind your back. A lack of freedom is frustrating. Yet, ironically, we usually can only blame ourselves because we designed most of our obligations and limitations via decisions.

FREEDOM AS A DIVIDEND FROM GOOD DECISIONS

The dividends of Free Time, Good Health, and Money combine to create Freedom. So, freedom is a result of several dividends that come from good decisions. Here is a good example of a freedom dividend from education level:

> **Thirty-nine percent of workers with a bachelor's degree worked from home on an average day in 2014. They were more than twice as likely as workers who attended college but didn't earn a bachelor's to enjoy this flexibility. Only 14 percent of high school graduates and 12 percent of workers without a high school diploma worked from home on an average day.[7]**

....

7 "Here's How Americans Spend Their Working, Relaxing and Parenting Time," Leah Libresco, FiveThirtyEight, June 24, 2015, http://fivethirtyeight.com/datalab/heres-how-americans-spend-their-working-relaxing-and-parenting-time/.

MOMENTUM AS AN INGREDIENT OF GOOD DECISIONS

"One way to keep momentum going is to have constantly greater goals."

—MICHAEL KORDA

"Momentum as an ingredient of good decisions: Success requires first expending ten units of effort to produce one unit of results. Your momentum will then produce ten units of results with each unit of effort."

—CHARLES J. GIVENS

Pause and consider for you: What does momentum feel like? When do you experience it? Say, for example, you are having a great weekend and one nice experience follows another. Does that momentum result in noticeable relaxation? Similarly, you'll notice when the workday is cruising along without unexpected disruption, the day's momentum puts a positive light on the day. Momentum feels good. Interestingly, we feel momentum the most when the brakes are applied suddenly. As we lurch to an uncomfortable stop, we know momentum has ceased.

Professional athletes get on a "streak." Golden State Warriors basketball guard Klay Thompson set a playoff record with eleven three-pointers in Game 6 of the 2016 Western Conference Finals against my Oklahoma City Thunder. He single-handedly destroyed OKC with his momentum, and he finished with forty-one points. Because he had momentum, the next shot was easier to take. That is the value of momentum as an ingredient in decision making. It's not logical or strategic—it's a condition.

One of the best ways to start momentum is to notice it. Give yourself credit on an hourly and daily basis for momentum you have created. People achieving weight-loss goals create momentum on a meal-by-meal and exercise-by-exercise basis. It all adds up. So, make momentum one of your ingredients.

MOMENTUM AS A DIVIDEND FROM GOOD DECISIONS

When we make good decisions, we experience the dividend of confidence and we create personal momentum. It's validation that we are doing the right things. Momentum is an essential ingredient that affects what we will attempt next. Momentum should be used on the next decision. Like a surfer riding a wave, the key is to first get on the wave and balance, and then the ride can begin.

JOY AS AN INGREDIENT OF GOOD DECISIONS

> *"Sometimes your joy is the source of your smile, but sometimes your smile can be the source of your joy."*
>
> —THICH NHAT HANH

We walk the earth carrying a varied amount of joy. The levels go up and down based upon who we are with, what we are accomplishing, and our sense of satisfaction at the moment. As an ingredient, joy serves as internal motivation to make a good decision. It's simple: We want more. We crave it when we don't have it. The most important thing about joy in a decision is the question: "Will this choice bring me joy later?" If we are making a decision affecting someone else, the question becomes, "Will this choice bring them joy later?" It is a human fact that we don't stick with things that don't bring us joy in some form. That is why joy is such an important ingredient.

JOY AS A DIVIDEND FROM GOOD DECISIONS

My grandmother's most joyful moment was listening for the family's happy delight in the wonderful meals she would create. The food tasted so good it was impossible not to make the point: Her cooking was fantastic. Our feedback created her dividend; it brought her joy.

> **Helping Others—An Automatic Dividend Creator**
>
> When we make a decision to donate something or donate our time to help someone, we are sowing the seeds of joy dividends. Not every decision yields time, health, money, or freedom. But when we are unselfish and helping someone, the dividend of joy is nearly certain, and it is one of the best feelings in the world.

Our decisions, when revealed as good ones, create that same feeling. We are the cook, so we await word that what we decided was good. It is affirming, assuring, and fun to see positive results from our decision-making skills.

We all make good decisions now and then and we achieve dividends. Let's prove it by looking at a few of your own examples. Recognizing your previous good work is important.

PERSONAL EXERCISE:
My Greatest Dividends and the Decisions That Got Me There

Using the categories below to brainstorm, identify five of the best decisions you have made so far in your life. For each of the five best decisions you have made so far in your life, write one or more dividends (choosing from the Big 6) after each of your examples. Your dividend labels should be easy to assign. If you have to think about it, it may not apply. For this important exercise, please make a handwritten response. Perhaps use a separate sheet of paper to record your thoughts.

Big 6 Dividends: Money, Time, Health, Freedom, Momentum, Joy

Note: A good decision does not have to be big.

DECISION CATEGORIES:

Money	Opportunities	Legal
Romance	Health	Family
Education	Purchases	Curiosity
Career / Business	Friendships	Where to live

Best Decision #1:	Dividend(s):
Best Decision #2:	Dividend(s):
Best Decision #3:	Dividend(s):
Best Decision #4:	Dividend(s):
Best Decision #5:	Dividend(s):

For illustration, I will use my personal examples.

Best Decision #1: Finishing college degree	Dividend(s): Momentum, Money
Best Decision #2: Marrying a good partner	Dividend(s): Joy, Momentum
Best Decision #3: Having children	Dividend(s): Joy
Best Decision #4: Starting my own business	Dividend(s): Freedom, Time, Money
Best Decision #5: Commitment to staying fit	Dividend(s): Health, Freedom

The important point here is to recognize that good decisions bring dividends, and you have already done that successfully. As we work through this book, we want to raise our personal expectations that the majority of our decisions can be good decisions, thus increasing dividends!

·9·

YOUR NEW TOOLKIT

Now that we have dealt with the past, we can prepare for our future. In this future we will be using some new tools. Every good craftsman needs the proper tools. You are building your future, so we will now give you the tools to make the most of it.

Setting Goals and Resetting Goals

I am standing in Walgreens in the massive candy aisle. It never fails that I think I know what I want heading into the store, but my mind begins to race as I am presented with so many choices. What am I craving right now? What haven't I had in a while? What is healthier for me? What candy will I regret least tomorrow? I am paralyzed by a decision. In my worst mindset, I avoid choosing by buying multiple items. That is hardly a disciplined approach! I am human too.

However, for a few key areas of our life, we must make firm choices. What are those key areas and how do we choose? We are answering these questions by learning some life tools that will hopefully be our north-south-east-west steady guide points as we navigate decisions.

"There is no such thing as work-life balance.
Everything worth fighting for unbalances your life."
—ALAIN DE BOTTON

Tool #1: Keep a Few Key Goals Close

One of my early mentors used to keep Post-it notes on his bathroom mirror, one for each goal he had at the time. When I would visit his house, the mirror was sometimes fifty percent covered in good intentions. Everything was started and yet nothing was finished. That's how he lived. Yet he was passionate about only a few key goals, and he would talk about them most often. It takes discipline to ignore the noise and focus on only a few key goals. When we focus, things get done.

"Pay daily attention to what you want to see grow."

If your goals were houseplants, how many could you water, fertilize, and manage daily? Perhaps you have too many "plants" and all of them are wilting! Our minds cannot simultaneously track more than a few "important" things. Therefore, we've got to narrow it down if we want good decision-making discipline. We must set **Prime Goals**.

PERSONAL EXERCISE:
My Prime Goals

For this important exercise, please make a handwritten response. Perhaps use a separate sheet of paper to record your thoughts that come to mind for each category.

Today's Date: ___/___/______

Categories: Career, love, money, education, travel, experiences, relationships, debt, health

As of today, my top five Prime Goals are

Category: Goal:
How I will measure progress:

Category: Goal:
How I will measure progress:

Category: Goal:
How I will measure progress:

Category: Goal:
How I will measure progress:

Category: Goal:
How I will measure progress:

Keep Prime Goals in Front

What can you do to keep these five Prime Goals in front of you at all times? Keeping a list on your phone is a simple method. Post-it notes on your bathroom mirror work, too! The most important thing is to keep your top goals in front of you. This first tool allows tools #2 and #3 to be possible. Also, after achieving one of these goals, replace it with a more appropriate one.

Tool #2: There's Only One #1

Too many goals dilute the significance of the most important goals. It's like too many friends make it difficult to have a few deep friendships. A handful of goals, like a small herd of horses, can be watched, managed, cared for, and enjoyed. If the herd gets too large, it becomes an awful chore and we become overwhelmed. I am often haunted by goals I carry around and for which I have made no progress. They follow me around like ugly luggage. They make me feel inadequate every time I think of them. So, let's maintain our Prime Goal short list (which you created as Tool #1), keeping it simple and begin using this second new tool: "There's only one #1."

I discovered this tool when I was advising a married couple who were unable to get pregnant after years of trying. They were in their mid-thirties and becoming very concerned. Obviously, "having a family" was a primary goal for them. I inquired about what they had been doing the past several years and quickly found the problem: They had too many goals, and none of their goals was labeled #1. *There can be only one overriding goal to which all other goals are second.* In their case, they were growing their own business, working sixty hours a week, remodeling a house in their free time, and she was skipping meals and also working out regularly, as fitness was important to her. This was their top five list of goals (not in any order):

- Growing their business
- Remodeling the house
- Starting a family
- Staying fit
- Saving money

It turned out that if she didn't work so many hours, she would also reduce their income, so the business growth and money saving goals would suffer. I told them, "It's time to choose a #1, and it doesn't have to harm your other goals for long." It was a stunning revelation to them that they had it backward. Their stated #1 concern was starting a family—yet their behavior and decisions did not support that #1 Prime Goal. With "family" selected as #1, I instructed them to design their world with decisions that made the #1 goal obvious and more likely to be achieved. She began working only half days, ate more calories while working out less intensely, began shutting down her day after nine p.m. (instead of remodeling)—and voila, they were pregnant in three months. Their decisions now supported their #1 goal.

PERSONAL EXERCISE:
My #1 Goal

For this important exercise, please make a handwritten response. Perhaps use a separate sheet of paper to record your thoughts. Complete this exercise for your #1 Prime Goal by choosing from the five Prime Goals listed above:

Today's Date: ____/____/________

As of today, my #1 goal is:

Category: Goal:

How I will measure progress:

You Can Change #1

Your #1 goal can change as you make progress with it. Other goals perhaps become more important. I know from my experience that my career goal of being a successful entrepreneur was #1 until I made notable progress—and then I outgrew the goal. Similarly, when a romantic goal is #1 and a person finds a great partner, they outgrow that goal. We achieve, we outgrow, and we advance other goals to be #1. That is the process.

OVERRIDING RULE

A #1 goal always gets favorable treatment. Nothing is allowed to hinder progress toward the top goal. All other goals are to be adjusted to make room for the top goal.

The odds of you achieving your top goal with this tool are much greater because you are promoting and defending the objective most important to you. It's bound to make progress.

Tool #3: Detecting Goal and Decision Overlap

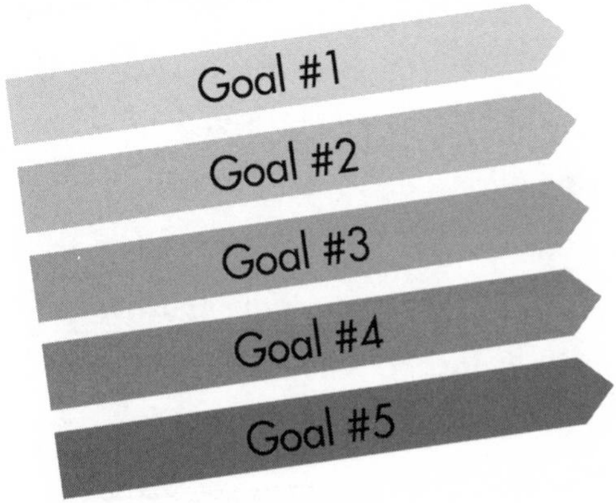

Being mindful of your top five goals is important in daily life because decisions will present themselves that "overlap" with the goals and potentially *help* or *hurt* your progress.

Some decisions are trivial, like what to wear today or eat for dinner. Other decisions are important—but they may not have an impact upon a primary goal.

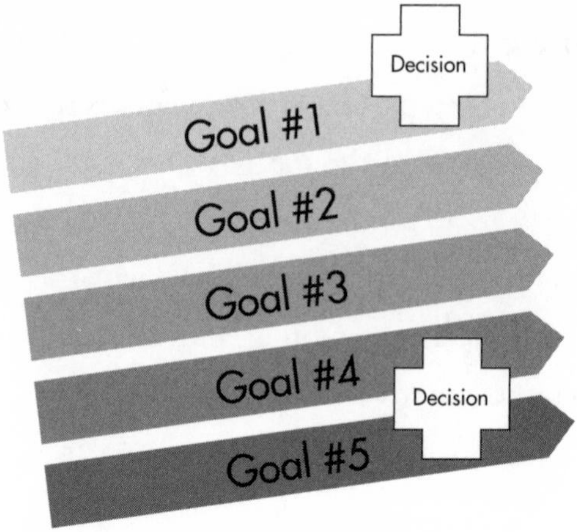

When a decision overlaps a Prime Goal, it becomes a **Prime Decision**. It is important to detect Prime Decisions. Awareness of Prime Decisions should raise your heart rate—you are on stage. This is now a significant decision—not because of the options in front of you—but because this choice can affect a significant goal. In other words, ***a decision's potential impact upon your life goals is what makes it significant.*** When you detect a goal/decision overlap, you now know to move forward with more caution because you are aware and are defending your goals above all else.

So, seemingly small/mid-sized decisions are now significant when an overlap is present.

> *Example 1*: If my goal is to advance in my career, the decision of whether to tell my employer, "I'll be on vacation during this critical project" becomes easy to decide. My decision is, "No, I won't be going on vacation because I am defending a primary goal re: my career." I am not suggesting vacation is to be

avoided—but if your absence comes at a critical time in which you can prove yourself, you have to make the choice to defend your goal. Your next promotion may depend upon it.

Example 2: If my goal is to win the heart of this particular girl and there is a chance she will be attending tonight's event, then I should decide to be at that same event (taking a chance she won't show) instead of joining my buddies who are hounding me to come with them. Gotta take a chance in love.

Example 3: If my goal is to stay off of diabetic drugs by watching my diet and losing weight—per my doctor's serious urging—I should decline an invitation to take a seven-day cruise. Floating atop the sea with twenty-four-hour buffets and strawberry daiquiris for a week could do serious damage to my momentum. My glucose levels will thank me.

Example 4: If my goal is to buy a house, then I should resist the urge to trade in my current car for the payment plan on the shiny new car. The extra cash can help me reach the goal sooner and my credit will be in better shape.

On and on we can think of examples where Prime Decisions must be detected because of their impact on our primary goals. Be proud of yourself when you connect the dots for Tool #3. You will detect several Prime Decisions *per day* if you are vigilant.

Tool #4: Recognizing Momentum

Have you ever had this feeling? I'm driving my car and beginning a downhill stretch of highway. I take my foot off the accelerator and smugly think, "I'm not using any gas right now" as my car's digital gauge displays "99 mpg." It's quieter as I coast downhill. I feel good about the moment. I noticed it! It reminds me that gravity works.

Your decision-making momentum deserves to be noticed, too. When you enjoy benefits of good decisions, it's unfair to not recognize and appreciate them as the dividends of your hard work as a decision maker. You may be on a good Decision Streak and it feels great. It's important to recognize momentum, as it reinforces what you are practicing about your goals and your decisions in life.

> *Example 1*: People with weight-loss goals desperately need to notice momentum to reinforce their new eating and exercise habits and to reprogram their brain's cravings. Noticing daily that they feel a little better, their clothes fit a little better, a compliment from a friend, the weight scale is lower, the energy level is higher . . . these are great indicators of momentum achieved by many decisions working together for a common goal: being healthier.

> *Example 2*: A good friend was single and looking for his soul mate. He was middle-aged, so it was a little more difficult to meet single women. He knew it was a matter of time and numbers—the more candidates he could meet per week would shorten the time to find a mutual match.

Therefore, he tracked his momentum by counting how many introductory meetings he could achieve per week, coordinating to meet at the local coffee shops because coffee was much faster (and cheaper) than lunch. Did I mention that he was socially awkward? Yet, with momentum he noticed weekly, within four months he achieved his goal and I was best man at his wedding.

Example 3: When we are looking to build savings/investment portfolios as a primary goal, we are rewarded by frequently looking at our account balances. The account balances show us the momentum for this goal and remind us why we make the decisions we make to spend wisely, make more, and save more. Regarding money, our decisions can support only one of two primary approaches, per Robert Kiyosaki, the author of *Rich Dad, Poor Dad*, who wrote:

> "The difference between my poor dad and my rich dad essentially came down to how they managed their money. Poor dad said, 'Live below your means.' My poor dad's budget or money management focused on cutting expenses to meet his income. [Alternatively] Rich dad said, 'Expand your means.' My rich dad's plan focused on increasing income. He said, 'Most people use their budget as a plan to become poor or middle class rather than to become rich. My budget is a plan to become rich.'"

Example 4: I am an experienced entrepreneur and I still haven't mastered the value of recognizing momentum when building a new business. I am the visionary and I stress about the "whole" effort being complete—yet that isn't an organized way to monitor progress. For example, if I were opening a new restaurant, I should create organized phases: (1) facility build-out, (2) purchasing equipment, (3) installation, (4) permits, (5) menu, (6) staff, (7) operating policy and training, (8) marketing, etc. As my efforts are phased, my momentum can be tracked and I can feel good about my progress toward my overriding goal of "Grand Opening."

Summary of Four Key Tools

When we combine what we have learned about decision making *and* adopt these four tools above, we are in a fantastic position to *operate* daily as a good decision maker:

1. Keep your Prime Goals close so you can manage them well.
2. Choose only one #1 Prime Goal to guarantee you achieve it.
3. Detect Prime Goal and decision overlap so you focus on the Prime Decision.
4. Recognize momentum toward your goals to reinforce your efforts.

Now we will transition to operating with your new personal power in your daily decision making.

·10·

PUTTING IT ALL TOGETHER—IN THE ACT

Now let's discuss how we operate in daily life as a good decision maker. Do you think you know how?

As a comparison, if I asked you, "Do you know how to operate as a good automobile driver in daily life?" would you confirm? Of course. You are licensed to drive and you have had lots of practice.

For decision making, we aren't licensed and we aren't well-practiced in our new discipline. Let's change the comfort level so it comes naturally.

What You Bring to the Moment

WHEN YOU GET OUT OF BED TOMORROW,
YOU CAN SAY THE FOLLOWING:

- I understand the impact my decisions have on my life (chapter 1).

- I understand that only a handful of decisions will affect the biggest of my life's goals, occurring in specific life phases (chapters 3, 4).
- I understand that sometimes I am The Decisionator, and that leads to bad decisions, pain, and more bad decisions (chapters 6, 7).
- I have made bad decisions in the past and have regrets because of those decisions. I have also seen dividends from my good decisions (chapters 7, 8).
- I have defined my current top goals (chapter 9).

Therefore, you are bringing all this good stuff with you to each moment that may require a decision. You are ready to defend your goals and not take a step backward with a bad decision (what *not* to do). Now, let's add some skills that will help you determine what *to do*.

The Good News and the Big Three

You don't have to remember everything to avoid screwing up your future. The good news is that you can walk the earth aware of only three things and you will benefit greatly. It's like never leaving home without $3 in your pocket. Always carry these three things and you can feel more confident. The three biggest things to remember (and practice) so you are always ready to focus upon a decision appropriately are—

1. Know Your Goals

Be aware of your primary goals. Know them by heart and review them often.

2. Pause

Recognize and then pause briefly on every decision. Ask yourself if a decision overlaps a primary goal. If so, it gets special consideration.

3. Eliminate Emotion

Be aware of your mental, physical, and emotional state so you recognize when you are The Decisionator. If you resemble that bad action hero, pause until you are no longer a menace to your future.

In the Act: Giving a Decision Special Consideration

In the popular game show *Who Wants to Be a Millionaire?* the game's creators designed the entire game around decision making. It wasn't just about getting the right answer to each question. Between questions was the bigger decision of whether the contestant should keep the current winnings or press forward, risking all the money earned thus far. The movie *Slumdog Millionaire* is an Academy Award–winning illustration of the emotional anguish when making decisions about life and that game show.

When a contestant was not certain of the answer to a question, they had three lifelines available:

- 50/50 (computer removes two of four possible answers)
- Ask the audience via survey
- Phone-a-friend

The use of these "lifelines" was dramatic and took extra TV time for careful evaluation. The contestant "knew" they needed to use a lifeline when they could only guess at the answer.

When you detect decision overlap with a Prime Goal, you "know" to give the Prime Decision special consideration. Never decide quickly. Your choice can make or break your momentum and possibly disrupt achieving your Prime Goal.

Your *immediate lifeline* is to take the pressure off of this moment. You can quickly use these phrases to create space for more thinking:

"Excuse me for a minute."

"I need a moment."

"I will call/email you later and let you know."

"I need to sleep on it."

"Can I get back to you on this?"

"When is the latest I can get back to you on this?"

After buying more time (minutes, hours, days, or weeks), your second lifeline is to simply think. Review the affected goal, its priority, and consider the impact of each possible option.

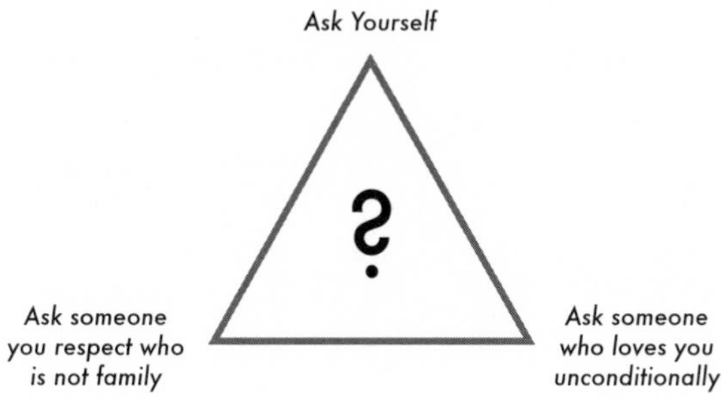

Decision Triangulation

If you still aren't certain about what decision is best, your third lifeline is doing the Decision Triangulation. To use this tool accurately, you must provide everyone involved with enough helpful information, not emotion. They will help you. Triangulate and trust the GPS accuracy and move forward.

In the Act: Know When You Are The Decisionator

Do you think lonely people make bad relationship decisions?
Do you think angry people tend to choose the wrong words?
Do you think prideful people hurt themselves and others?
Yes. Yes. Yes.

We see it every day: people at key moments not ready for that moment and doing damage to their future.

As you are pausing to give a decision special consideration, do not contaminate the result because you are The Decisionator. From chapter 6, we discovered that we are often unfairly tainting our decisions because we have one or more of the following traits at the moment:

Desperate	Angry	Depressed
In a Hurry	Rejected/Lonely	Fear/Grief
Prideful	Tired/Fatigue	
Egocentric	Hope/Optimism	

Before you start working on the decision, ask yourself, "How do I feel?" If you are carrying any of the above traits at the moment, pause even longer and deal with The Decisionator first.

Do not return to the decision until you have lost The Decisionator persona.

Antidotes to The Decisionator

If you are:

IN A HURRY

Stop and ask, "What's the hurry?" Remind yourself that fast deals are never the best deals. In fact, a rushed decision creates anxiety—which we don't need either.

PRIDEFUL

You are concerned right now with your self-worth, your self-importance. You cannot cash those. In this case, take inventory of what you are thankful for. Thinking about the people and animals and blessings in our lives quickly restores a lovable and balanced humility to our human condition.

EGOCENTRIC

Stop thinking about how you appear to others. You are about to "cut off your nose to spite your face." Discard any thoughts of how you appear and, instead, get selfish. Ask yourself while ignoring all others, "What's in my best long-term interests right now?" and just do it.

ANGRY

Shut up until you're calm. Think about what you are going to say before you say it. Breathe deeply like a sniper, in and out to lower your heart rate. Leave the room. Exercise. Brainstorm other options. Use humor. Forgive. People aren't perfect.

FEELING REJECTED/LONELY

You are dealing with bad news or feeling let down by someone important to you. Your sense of security has been threatened. You will first blame yourself, which may be incorrect. Remember, this isn't about you, it's about the other. You cannot change people. This happened for a greater reason. Consider only what value you can gain from this rejection to make yourself better and use it. Talk to friends and family who love you.

TIRED/FATIGUE

This is just bad timing. You happen to be lacking the energy to focus. Sleep and eat and recharge and you will be tip-top to make a decision.

FULL OF HOPE/OPTIMISM

This is the sneaky one. You are always hopeful for something better. The quick test is to review what you know to be the unpolished facts about your options. The quick antidote is to discard what you hope the options include and look at what you can prove right now.

DEPRESSED

Your emotions will swing from low to high and your decisions are vulnerable. We do instantly pleasurable things when depressed, and these can be self-destructive. This is not about you being weak. Depression is not only about attitude, perspective, or wanting things to be different. It is a chemical balance issue. You either have enough of a brain chemical or you don't. Avoid alcohol, exercise, and see your doctor.

DESPERATE

Don't give up. You haven't yet explored all options. You don't know what you don't control. In desperate situations a door can open we did not expect. Instead of analyzing the situation over and over, in this case, become still and let life introduce a way forward. You have a network of friends and family. Even strangers can do amazing things. Find some peace. Pray. Have faith in yourself. Let all the internal messaging from ego, pride, and fear die down so you can see and listen clearly.

FEELING FEAR OR GRIEF

Safety can be felt by being around family and close friends. Overarching fears/concerns as well as grief cannot be made to simply go away. Those feelings will revisit tomorrow. However, when we are needing to make a decision, invite someone who cares about you to join you and assist in the evaluation. Two heads are better than one in this case.

IN OTHER WORDS

Summarizing from the other direction, if you can tell yourself, "I am not The Decisionator at this moment," then you are likely to make a good decision.

A Real Case Study for "Putting it all Together"

A thirty-two-year-old professional wrote me:

I am looking for some guidance and clarity on how to best evaluate my options. My contract at my firm expires in early June of next year and I am at an inflection point of my career. I feel like the next step/decision I make will likely be the path I choose for the next ten to twenty years and this is weighing heavily on me. I have had both a positive/negative experience in my current role which has been the last seven years. There are a few different options that lie ahead of me: (1) stay where I am and try and negotiate a restructuring of how our team operates, (2) try and separate myself from my team and operate solo, (3) move within the firm to a different city, (4) move to a different firm and continue in the same line of work I am doing now (sales side) or get into a different side of the business (principal side). I'm looking to establish a clearly defined thought process to evaluate each option and determine the best option to choose.

Using the principles of this book, I responded:

This is a common situation as a career accelerates. Yet, you are bogged down with discussing options: Work at this company or that company/Work with these people or those people/Work in this role or another role/Be an employee or self-employed/Work in this city or that city, etc. This suggests to me that you have no gravitational pull of personal primary goals helping you focus on decision options that can attain those goals. Once you define Prime Goals and define a priority, your options will fall into place and you will know what to do.

People flounder when they don't link their decision options to their Prime Goals for their life. That is where the work is. It doesn't work (as we get older) to just have intentions to be generally successful—you will be generally satisfied with accomplishments that never fulfill any desires. We must frame the decision-making process with what we truly want in the future. You need to answer these questions for yourself:

- What work role do I like the best and see myself doing well and enjoying for the next ten years (what is my goal for my daily work role)?
- In what city do I want to work and live and enjoy? What weather do I want to feel every day or what seasons do I want to have every year?
- Do I have a career goal? If so, what is it specifically?
- Do I have an income goal as a primary goal? If so, what is it specifically?
- What kind of company do I want to work for? What about the company satisfies a goal of mine?
- Where do I want my challenge to come from: team accomplishments (growing managerial skills) or individual task accomplishments (growing task skills)?
- What is my favorite hobby, and where and how is that hobby most supported?

And then, from the options you have, which options remain viable when you apply your answers to the above?

After that, you can ask these questions to narrow down your options:

- What decision option can deliver a majority of your goals from above?
- What decision option best fits your personal relationships/family?
- What decision option gets you most excited?

- If no option is a clear winner, ask: What decision options have I not considered yet that could be a better fit? Widen the options scope—this could involve a career pivot.

Note: If the majority of the above goals cannot be clearly attainable by working for someone else, then you are a good fit for considering forming your own company—because at least you have a chance to attain your goals without constraints from other belief systems.

Last, if goals cannot help this decision right now because they are unclear or not fitting the decision, you can perform the consequences exercise:

1. List each possible option (e.g. Option A: Stay in current company in current position in current city).
2. For each of your options, list the consequences you think are likely if you choose that option and stay with it for at least five years.
3. For now, choose the option that has the consequences you can most accept when compared to all the other options.

My conclusion: I hope this is helpful. To break through, we have to step back and focus on ourself, our life, what we want out of our life, and what we want in addition to a career (balance).

·11·

WHEN DECISIONS GO BAD

"Shallow men believe in luck or in circumstance.

Strong men believe in cause and effect."

—RALPH WALDO EMERSON

Kaboom! There goes a decision we made long ago or at the last minute. Medic! We screwed up. The pain approaches: My anxiety has turned to regret. I am certain I made a bad decision. The consequences lurk in my future. What now? Given enough time, nearly every bad decision we make is revealed to us with a twisted smile. Sometimes, it takes years (of marriage, of career, of employment, of purchase, of debt, etc.). Other times, it takes seconds (wrong turn, first bite of dinner, saying the wrong thing, texting while driving, overdose, etc.). It's just a matter of time and the bad decision indicators sprout like yellow dandelions in springtime.

Knowing why bad decisions happen doesn't prevent us from making them. We're human and we tend to learn the hard way sometimes, right? So, even though we are gaining some new decision-making tools, we can also better understand and deal with those instances when we discover a decision-gone-bad.

Why is it critical to apply a tourniquet to a bleeding limb? Answer: to stop the bleeding and be alive for the next opportunity. In decision making, it's important that we stop the damage and improve whatever we can improve. A quick and correct decision post-failure can reduce future regret significantly. How we react is critical because the wrong action could irreparably harm your larger goal. Have you ever shouted the insult and left the room in front of a slamming door? That door slam could also be the sound of your goal crashing to the floor—forever. If we are prepared with the strategies in this chapter, we can feel confident in our decision making post-failure. Let's review the nature of our reactions to "bad decisions revealed" and ways we can improve our perspective.

Good Choices When Confronting a Bad Decision

How do we know a decision has gone bad? Usually, there is proof before our eyes. As discussed earlier, our anxiety about that decision quickly turns into regret when we have proof. What happens to us in that moment when we must accept and deal with this realization?

There are three good things we must try to do when dealing with a bad decision failure:

1. Control the mental chaos in our heads and think clearly.
2. Make a solid second (reactionary) decision to minimize the long-term damage.
3. Avoid deflecting the real cause of failure (attributing the failure to anything other than our decision-making ability in the past, or chance).

Mind Blown: Controlling the Mental Chaos

In a slow-motion video sequence, focusing upon our inner working forces, there is a complex series of mental and physical reactions when we must admit we were wrong and decide what to do about it. The pressure is high in a firefight of internal finger-pointing while seeking relief. Bad decisions revealed put us under stress. ***When under stress, our minds work differently*** and we cannot control our natural tendencies to react and cope. In formally testing my tendencies, I learned that under business stress I quickly resort to anger. That explained a lot over the years, actually. Another experience was a few years ago when I went through a multiday terrorist defense assault rifle certification course with a bunch of ex-soldiers (I was the only non-soldier). I am a good shot at most yardages—but that was not the point to this grueling course.

For four days, we were subjected to high-stress shooting decision making while wearing eighty pounds of gear in the hot Louisiana sun. That was stress, and my decision making was initially quite flawed. I learned for certain that adrenaline was my enemy when I needed to think. Combat stress introduced fear, and fear introduced adrenaline. "Fight or flight" mental and physical reactions were not designed to also include rational thinking. This is why some police officers have made mistakes and taken action they regret with crime suspects immediately following a chase or confrontation. They are not in control of their decision making while under stress, pumped full of adrenaline. This takes a lot of training and unfortunately can ruin a career if not mastered because the results can be fatal. Being confronted with a bad decision we've made can incite fear, and then we can react poorly because we are angry or pumped up with adrenaline. The mind is chaotic in these moments, and we should notice all the different internal messages and learn which ones to ignore for the moment when under duress.

THE PLAYERS IN THE HEAT OF THE MOMENT

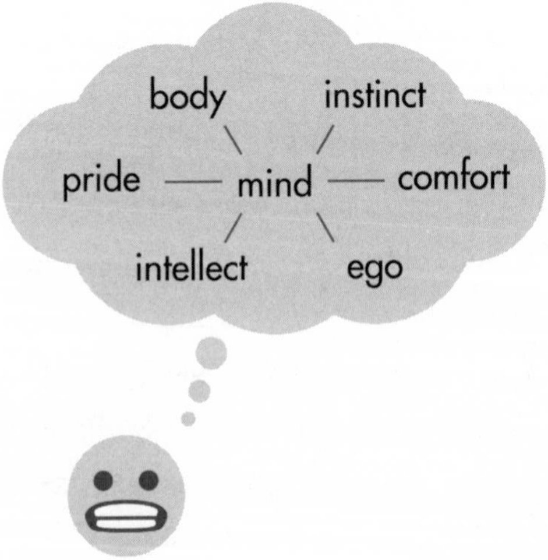

Your awareness of the battle going on in your head is critical to confronting a bad decision. If you understand to whom you should listen and whom you should "hush!" in your thinking chaos, you will have the advantage in reacting to a bad decision.

Mind: Our mind is the referee. It tries to manage an outcome. It needs to be clear and focused to do its best work.

Instincts: Our instincts (gut feelings) speak early, but denial renders them mute. What good are instincts when denial is master? Instincts remain permanently on record with their early recommendation.

Ego: How we appear to others is extremely important to us. Thus, that ego will want to postpone embarrassment as long as possible because it fails to quantify the amount of total embarrassment. Ego practically bullies all the other players to avoid looking bad.

Intelligence: Intelligence is the problem solver, searching for the optimal solution. When partnered with ego, our intellect (for a moment) thinks it can find a shortcut (get away with the error). Intellect, when corrupted, begins working on the best way to solve the problem *and* satisfy ego—which rarely works out. (See Alec Baldwin's multiple failures with the media.)

Body: Our bodies try to avoid stress. Stress brings fatigue, and fatigue enables bad decision making. So, the weakened body will undercut a strong mind and just want a decision to be made.

Pride: Our pride is built from our successes. The more successful we have been, the harder it is to convince pride to take the hit right now. Pride will always want to delay consequences—even if it hurts more in the long term.

Comfort: We long to be comfortable in mind and body. Discomfort feels bad, and we are programmed to find comfort. Seeking comfort is a form of "taking shelter" in a storm. It is not a long-term answer. Unfortunately, recognizing a bad decision creates a storm—and we will often choose what is comfortable instead of what is best for us long term.

A Bad Decision Reaction Illustrated in Milliseconds

Mind: "I just heard that we have a problem."

Instincts: "I told you so!"

Ego: "I don't hear anything."

Pride: "Wasn't me."

Body: "Where's the exit?"

Intelligence: "Where's the evidence?"

Mind: "All of you, shut up so I can think!"

Ego: "Nah. Who's hungry?"

Instincts: "We've got to deal with it."

Mind: "Assembling options . . ."

Comfort: "This is bad territory."

Body: "I'm starting to sweat."

Pride: "I don't make these types of mistakes."

Ego: "We are going to look really stupid."

Intelligence: "There is no fix—only quarantine options."

Pride: "It wasn't me that screwed this up."

Body: "I need to feel better right now!"

Ego: "I'm still beautiful."

Instincts: "Don't make any knee-jerk decisions."

Comfort: "Let's find a quick compromise that's familiar."

Intelligence: "The best option is to embrace the mistake fully."

Pride, Ego, Body [chorus]: "Oh no, that's too painful right now."

Mind: "I am driven by chemicals, and right now, the chorus is deafening."

Intelligence: "We are so screwed."

Right there. In just milliseconds, it is human to be suddenly vulnerable in the wake of a bad decision. We are suddenly ill at ease and forced to consider the worst outcome. Thus, at this moment of vulnerability, we have two options:

Option 1: Address the first (original) decision failure and consequences head-on, swiftly.

Option 2: Anything but option 1.

After enough (hard) experience flailing about with option 2, wisdom tends to push people toward option 1 as the best option.

Reaction: The Second Decision Opportunity

"Things are rarely as bad as they seem" is a common phrase at a low moment. I add to this phrase in this manner: "Things are rarely as bad now as they will be later if we fail to react appropriately and make a good second decision." Acknowledging and dealing head-on with the first bad decision is the second decision, our "reaction." If the second decision is poor, the overall cost can more than double. Thus, we have a big opportunity to get back on track with a good second decision. Then why don't we?

The Battle over a Second Decision

In the following examples, think about the struggle among different interests in the consequences game: mind, instinct, intelligence, body, ego, and pride.

Imagine what would have happened differently to Richard Nixon if he had said early, "Yes, I screwed up and went along with a plan to gain information about my opponent. It was stupid, I didn't think it through, it violated someone's constitutional rights, and I am deeply sorry. I will not condone a cover-up, and we will get to the bottom of this." He might have been impeached, but he wouldn't have had to resign disgraced via the Supreme Court ruling against him—taking the public's trust down with him.

Similarly, consider how Bill Clinton would have fared if he had not chosen denial of an affair with a White House intern, but instead said, "I regret to acknowledge that I made a very poor decision. I am sorry for this coming to light as your president. I owe the greatest apology to my wife and will be working to save my marriage from this point forward." He would never have had to do a deposition and would never have been impeached by the House of Representatives, and the issue would have been over in months instead of years.

Have you ever postponed a breakup of any kind (romantic, friend, work) because you had all the evidence you needed but breaking up the relationship just didn't happen? There are several possible reasons for this result, and these errors are defined below.

Personally, I have been in the business position to call a business that a partner and I had purchased a loss—but we refused to do it. Had we acknowledged it early, the loss would have been a half million dollars. Denial pushed the cost up to $3 million two years later. How does this happen? I can tell you that decision bias grows bigger as long as you let it grow—like a snowball rolling downhill. The longer you deny the decision failure, the bigger the failure gets. In this business deal, the numbers looked shaky in the beginning, so we researched/planned why it would work. With that satisfactory false buffer, we moved the factory operation from Philadelphia to Chicago—an expensive move involving twenty-five semitrucks. We relocated some employees. We spent a ton of money moving fifteen machines that had sat on the Philadelphia factory floor for twenty years, adjusted perfectly. When we moved that equipment, it wasn't a simple matter to put it back together and make it work. The equipment didn't work like it used to. We reasoned it was just a matter of time and adjustments. Yet it was also missing the machine operator who knew to kick the tire before flipping the switch, etc. We downplayed the idea that we had bought worn-out equipment. We chased our tails, and all the while the Chinese and Indians were willing to make these products for less money than we could make them in Chicago. Gee whiz, that hurt. But I learned a great lesson—you can always pull the emergency brake and stop the train. In fact, the earlier we do it, the less damage done.

You may have a bad decision in your past that you ignored and the problem grew bigger. Have you ever wondered why we fail to make the right call at the time?

The Heroes in a Good Second Decision

If we serve Mind, Instinct, and Intellect first, we can make a good second decision. This requires us to ignore ego and pride while examining our goals and what we really want for a result.

Thus, when dealing with a bad decision, we benefit by remembering to keep a clear mind, listen early to our instincts, and let our intellect work without being corrupted by ego and pride. If we follow this prescription, our body will undergo less stress and we will have a better long-term result.

The Villains of a Bad Second Decision

The usual suspects prevent us from reacting correctly. Before we accept responsibility for our decision making and react logically, we often look for an escape—a way to avoid dealing directly with our decision failure. These are convenient and easy escape options. Perhaps that is why society uses them so broadly at great cost. Let's look a little closer to sharpen our actions when our bad decisions are revealed to us.

We potentially err in four categories. Each category carries its own damage.

ERROR	DAMAGE
Deflection	Costly delays due to no real action/solution
Defending Sunk Cost	Further bad investment
Accepting the Unacceptable	Violating our personal standards
Goal Grooming	Downgrading our future

ERROR: Deflecting the Real Cause of a Bad Decision

"It hurts, because we wanted a different outcome, but then we make it hurt even worse by creating a narrative around what happened. So, instead of creating that debilitating narrative, I think we're better served realizing that now, we have an opportunity to pivot—to take our life in a different direction."

—CHRIS HILL

Failing is painful. Sometimes it is too painful to acknowledge accurately. People in our society prefer to point the finger at anything or anyone but themselves. We are skilled at finding automatic scapegoats toward which we deflect responsibility when a bad decision has made its mark. We must avoid the following forms of deflection or we lose the opportunity to reach a conclusion. Have you ever used these?

DEFLECTION #1: IT WAS FATE

"It was fate . . ." offers your subconscious mind, suggesting that there was always a predetermined movie script for your life that involved you making a bad decision and then climaxes with you discovering how badly it turned out. This script also dictates the actions of all the people and things in your life that could have affected your circumstances and your thinking at the time of your decision—and the whole time since. How realistic is that? This kind of thinking, while convenient, doesn't help us. If we were to accept the idea of fate, then why even try to make a difference? ***Fate is a myth used by weak minds***, and its use prevents us from acknowledging a bad decision that we made and gaining wisdom by learning from it. If fate were real, then the script includes not only the consequences of a bad decision but also how you respond to it. Your response is exactly what this chapter is about. Be sure that you understand and fully accept the fact that the movie script of your life is being written and directed by you. Fate is a lazy myth.

DEFLECTION #2: BLIND FAITH

It's a pleasant notion to believe that "good things will come to those who wait"—but reality tells a different story. A bad decision reveals its consequence at a time you cannot choose. When this happens, we must deal with it. Having faith that "things will work out" is not action that advances our cause. Rather, it is inaction that is convenient and lazy. In fact, as a bad decision is being revealed, you may have an opportunity to limit the damage. It's all about your actions at the point you suspect things are not going the way you anticipated.

The concept of being a good victim because you are waiting patiently for the desired outcome is harmful. While you are waiting, the world is passing you by. In this "faith mode," if something good happens, it was simply coincidence, nothing more. Is coincidence a plan? Are you a good victim? Of course not! When a friend says "have faith" or "keep the faith," what are they really saying? Are they consoling our hurt feelings or suggesting a plan of action? I suggest that people try to respond positively because it makes them feel better and it's all they can offer. They don't know your situation well enough to really dig in. The real action is up to you.

We can tolerate the opinions of others, but we need to hold firm to personal truths about faith and optimism. We can believe in people, having faith that people generally try to do the right thing. We can have faith in God. We can have faith in a cause. However, that's where the usefulness of faith ends; we have no control of those things. The player sitting on the bench has faith that he/she will get into the game—while the others are in the game—playing, making it happen. Faith is not action. When we trip over a bad decision, we need to have confidence in ourselves and embrace the fact that the long-term consequences of this bad decision will be determined by our actions from this moment forward. We can make it better, or worse. We can learn from this or trip over it again in the future. Blind faith is a lazy victim's approach.

DEFLECTION #3: IT IS GOD'S WILL

This may raise some eyebrows, but I see people reaching for this escape too often. I do not intend to take a religious stance in this statement. Rather, I suggest that the concept of "God's will" is misunderstood and misused when we encounter the results of bad decisions. Probably the clearest example of the knee-jerk use of "God's will" is when someone dies too young and one or more people who knew that person will remark, "It was God's will." This suggestion irritates me because their statement can be rewritten as "God wanted this person to die at this time." Really? Shouldn't we look first at some really bad decision making? The five-year-old decided to run into the street; the forty-five-year-old decided to weigh three hundred pounds and have high cholesterol; Steve Irwin decided to face dangerous wild animals for the cameras; Walt Disney and Jesse Owens decided to be smokers; Jimi Hendrix, Marilyn Monroe, and Heath Ledger decided to be drug users; etc. In other words, it is not likely that God is spending energy to will (cause) you to make a bad decision when the majority of what the New Testament describes is His incredible love for us. Thus, it is the bad decision that causes consequences, not God's will.

The concept of God's will is documented in the Bible with varied interpretations of how much free will He provides the rest of us in our lives. John 10:17–18 quotes Jesus to say, "I lay down My life so that I may take it again. No one has taken it away from Me, but I lay it down on My own initiative. I have authority to lay it down, and I have authority to take it up again." Throughout the Bible, we can see that free will exists for each of us as to whether we choose sin or not (uphold His commandments or not), follow God or not, etc. Part of "flourishing" on this earth is we humans making the most of what He gives us, including great minds with which to learn and make good decisions. To attribute the consequences to God when you made the original decision is a copout. The same is true when you give Him the glory for a good outcome. If we want to be appreciative to Him for a good outcome from a decision we've made, it would be accurate to thank God for helping us be in a position to make a good decision, helping us obtain the needed ingredients for a good decision, but not the decision itself. We own our decisions, and we cannot assign them elsewhere when it feels convenient to do so. ***Decisions are our free will in action.***

> *"People always call it luck when you've acted more sensibly than they have."*
>
> —ANNE TYLER

DEFLECTION #4: "IT'S JUST BAD LUCK"

If you were to pull your car into the next convenience station and purchase a Powerball lottery ticket . . . and win . . . would you call that "good luck"? If you get back onto the highway and are driving behind a large truck and it throws a rock to crack your windshield, would you call that "bad luck"? What is luck? Is "Lady Luck" another name for "chance"? Yes, it is. Luck is randomness of the universe nearest you, acting and reacting in completely random fashion. You cannot create good luck or bad luck—it just happens. However, you can put yourself in position to benefit from randomness (or be hurt by it). By purchasing the lottery ticket, you put yourself in the position to win against incredible odds. By driving closely behind the large truck, you put yourself in the position to catch a rock in your windshield. Once you put yourself in any position, the results are random and the outcome is based upon probability, known also as the odds.

A Few Odds

The odds of becoming a lightning victim in the US in any one year is 1 in 700,000. The odds of being struck in your lifetime is 1 in 3,000.

In comparison, the odds of winning the Powerball lottery are 1 in 175,223,510 per ticket. Thus, we are 250 times *more* likely to be struck by lightning than to win the Powerball jackpot. Over a lifetime, assuming we bought a Powerball ticket every month for fifty years, we are 973 times *more* likely to be struck by lightning than to win the Powerball jackpot.

Star Wars: Episode V: The Empire Strikes Back
C-3PO: Sir, the possibility of successfully navigating an asteroid field is approximately 3,720 to 1!
Han Solo: Never tell me the odds.

The odds don't change to suit our needs. In the lottery of life, success or failure is about each of us controlling our *position*. If you put yourself in a high crime area, the odds are higher you will be "unlucky" with a criminal. If you wear your seatbelt, you will be more "lucky" in a car crash. If you graduate college, you greatly increase your odds of getting a good job. You cannot change the odds unless you can manipulate the ingredients. Thus, all you can really affect, on issues that are mostly chance (luck), is to put yourself in the best position to win.

At the Casino

As you sit at the Vegas blackjack table and the dealer is pulling cards from a six-deck shoe, there is nothing that you can do to (1) change the cards in that 312-card shoe; or (2) change the cards the other players take; or 3) change the cards the dealer takes. It's purely random and the odds are fixed. This is why card counting is illegal—because it changes the player's odds. Legally, you can only control your knowledge of the rules and winning strategies. Some players change tables! Fact: At any casino, the game odds are all against you (less than fifty percent). Thus, players know that if a lucky streak happens, walking away preserves the gain. Otherwise, you'll eventually give it all back to the house!

WHAT DOES THIS HAVE TO DO WITH BAD AND GOOD LUCK?

Have you ever heard someone say, "I ran into a streak of bad luck"? When bad luck happens, we must realize we put ourselves in position to make that possible. When good luck happens, we should note that we put ourselves in position to benefit from chance. What we should not do is fall prey to believing that luck is due to anything other than randomness or believing we had anything to do with creating luck—other than putting ourselves into position to benefit from it.

DID YOU KNOW?

Several psychology studies have shown that, in general, women tend to attribute their success to good luck while men attribute their success to their own skill. Conversely, women tend to attribute their failure to their own (lack of) skill while men attribute their failure to bad luck.

DEFLECTION #5: DENIAL—"IT'S NOT TRUE"

The president of the United States has, more than once, showed us the wisdom and stupidity of denying an allegation, attempting a cover-up, and finally admitting to the wrongdoing. A bad decision made years earlier can come to light, and a fast escape route is to double down with denial. From college football coaches to Hollywood starlets to local coffee shop regulars, the truth usually comes out about a bad decision, and they take the consequences to a new low with denial. False denial adds to your resume either "clueless" or "liar." In the business world, I see business owners all the time who are in financial denial about the condition of their businesses. They remain incredulous as their creditors are liquidating the business for pennies on the dollar. ***Ignorance is a choice.*** People either don't know (ignorance) or they know and refuse to acknowledge (denial) the results of bad decision making. Denial is only temporary. Reality finds us all eventually.

DEFLECTION #6: ACCOMMODATION— "I AM NOT TRYING HARD ENOUGH"

In my early management days, when I had evidence that an employee was a bad hire, I would double down. For a poor hire, I would spend more time with them, more clearly specifying what needed to be done, accommodating their quirks by adjusting their job description, whatever needed to be done to make them "work out OK." Thus, I would spend more time, more money, and opportunity cost to get to the same result: They departed the business anyway. We do this in dating relationships and marriage as well. Accommodation makes us feel recommitted to the relationship via the belief that the reason the relationship is not working must be due to our lack of effort or understanding. This belief is usually incorrect. The flaw is in the ingredients. Accommodation is too hard to sustain, and once the heroic effort stops, the real result appears again. To refresh this feeling, think about the last personal or work relationship you had that turned out to simply be too much work to hold together. Accommodation is draining and unsustainable.

PERSONAL QUIZ

What form of deflection do you most tend to use?

ERROR: Defending Sunk Costs—"I have too much invested to quit now"

This error is sort of like "going down with the ship" because you are a stubborn captain of the famous boat, USS *Failed Decision*. It is a common failure in second decision making to reflect upon all the cumulative effort and investment up to this moment and lament,

"I have worked at this so long," "I have invested so much," or "I have come too far to quit on this now . . ." An everyday example is the car you have had for ten years that has been reliable, but you have had to make expensive repairs lately and another big repair is needed now. The wrong consideration is the money you have spent on the car up to this moment. That is "sunk cost"—it is immaterial to this decision now. It doesn't matter what you have spent or how long you have owned the car. The correct consideration is how much value you are guaranteed in the future with this new repair vs. your alternative course of action. If the present value of the car, when fixed, is less than or equal to the cost of this new repair, you know it is a bad decision. Another common example involves two people in a dating relationship where one is happy and the other is not ("This isn't going anywhere"). The unhappy party is waiting for the other person to change, make a decision, commit, or succeed, and it is not happening as the clock is ticking on their lives. Yet, rather than take action, "We've been dating a long time" clouds the judgment of the unhappy person as he/she is defending a sunk cost. Don't deflect by considering your prior investments. All that matters are the benefits going forward among alternatives you have in this immediate fork in the road.

PERSONAL QUIZ

What is a current situation where I am defending a sunk cost and staying with it when I know I shouldn't?

ERROR: Accepting the Unacceptable

The damage-causing alternative to *deflection* is *acceptance* (with modifications). We are taught to compromise throughout our lives. Our parents teach us to "work it out" or "make compromises" to resolve differences between us and others. However, it is a huge mistake to compromise when it involves accepting what we previously labeled unacceptable. Our judgment is impaired at the moment of possible compromise, and we should not be reevaluating our prior determination. It's like rethinking your diet resolution with the ice cream sitting in front of you. Compromise of this type causes you damage. It is a tempting and convenient tactic to modify what we will accept in order to make what is available fit our needs and wants. Can you imagine compromising on your shoe size when shopping for dress shoes? A single size difference can bring a lot of pain for you as long as you wear those shoes. It is the same consequence for your future if you accept the unacceptable. You will come to your senses and regret it later.

A Dad's Advice

My friend's father is a behavioral psychologist. He gave her this advice:

For anything important, make a list of the things you want. Make a list of the things you don't want. You won't get everything you want. Do not settle for a single item on your list of things you don't want.

"Waiter, there's a fly in my soup!"

"It's OK, sir, there's no extra charge!"

Will you accept flies in your soup? We are vulnerable to this error when we are unprepared with the list of what we will not accept (see A Dad's Advice above). Creeping tolerance of unacceptable factors in an important area of our life is a slippery slope. We must be aware of the things we absolutely do not want. Examples:

"I will not accept attending college near my hometown."

"I will not accept living my entire adult life in the same place."

"I will not accept marrying a short man."

"I will not accept dating a smoker."

"I will not accept being an overweight person or being married to someone who is."

"I will not accept having debt."

"I will not accept a career working indoors/at a desk."

"I will not accept marrying someone who doesn't want children."

"I will not accept always worrying about my finances."

We should not compromise by Accepting the Unacceptable. You will be grateful tomorrow for having a strong backbone today.

PERSONAL EXERCISE: My Unacceptables

Thinking about what you want in your near future or long-term future, make a list of what you don't want—what is your list of unacceptables? For this important exercise, please make a handwritten response. Perhaps use a separate sheet of paper to record your thoughts.

ERROR: Goal Grooming

The saddest and worst reaction to a bad decision is to perform "Goal Grooming." We lose when we adjust our goals to fit the circumstances/current results.

"I didn't want that job anyway."

"I didn't really need to see Paris."

"Marriage/children doesn't have to happen for me."

"I don't have to get that specific degree."

"I'll guess I'll never be fit or thin."

"Owning a house is overrated."

"Instead of relocating to the city I desire,
I can just visit once in a while."

"I have been wanting a black SUV, but the dealer
only has blue. I guess I like blue, too."

It is a form of self-soothing to restate our goals to make the current failure feel less painful. We need to catch ourselves when we are Goal Grooming and perform a quiet pause—to let the pain subside and not negatively coach ourselves any further. It's "stinkin' thinkin'" to restate goals. Reduced goals are permanent course corrections and a reduction in life's rewards.

PERSONAL QUIZ:
Goals I've Groomed

What was the last goal I considered grooming downward? How did I react? For this important exercise, please make a handwritten response. Perhaps use a separate sheet of paper to record your thoughts.

Second Decision Option 1 of 2: Fail Fast

Instead of *deflection* and *defending sunk costs* and *Accepting the Unacceptable* and *Goal Grooming*, the better idea is this: Fail Fast, don't try to fix it . . . it's time to move on. You have all the evidence you need and it's OK to go fast (this isn't the same error as hurrying on a first decision). This is the second (reactionary) decision about what you are going to do with this specific failure. When it's time to deal with failure, do it quickly. Don't drag it out. It prolongs pain and creates possible opportunity costs (things you could have done instead, people you could have met instead). When we have ample evidence of failure from a past decision, it's time to act. A good second decision is to Fail Fast. It does not come naturally to us because failing has been labeled so dreadful. On the contrary! It is more dreadful to make the failure bigger and take longer to do so. To successfully Fail Fast, we do not make the errors as described above, as that will waste time, throw us off course, and distract us from what we really need: a conclusion and a restart.

To Fail Fast is not to quit. It is to stop adding to a poor investment.

Have you ever postponed failure and the result was the same anyway? What was the difference? Lost time, effort, and emotion. Life examples—

- Not breaking up when you know it's not going to work
- Not selling when you have an offer
- Not quitting the job when you know it's a dead end
- Not giving up spending when money is tight
- Not stopping the project when it is obviously not turning out correctly
- Not declining the invitation when you have no interest in the people inviting you

When Failing Fast, turn the guilt and fear into satisfaction that you have reached a conclusion and you can move on. Certainty feels good. "I'm done with that."

PERSONAL EXERCISE: A Failure on Life Support

What failure have I been keeping alive using the above errors when it deserves to Fail Fast so I can move forward positively? For this important exercise, please make a handwritten response. Perhaps use a separate sheet of paper to record your thoughts.

Second Decision Option 2 of 2: Fix Fast

The only alternative to *Failing Fast* is to *Fix Fast.* Yet Fixing Fast has one specific requirement or it cannot qualify as an alternative: The Fix must fundamentally change the situation, alter the terms, or rework the deal. The Fix cannot be to try harder, recommit, and rely upon good intentions or promises. The Fix is not a compromise. The Fix is a real, physical adjustment to the original failure. When we are waking up to a cold house in the winter, a Fix is to adjust the thermostat and start the heat. When it begins raining on us, a Fix is to take ourselves indoors. When we are unhappy with our group, a Fix is to change the group leader or leave the group. When we cannot get our work done, a Fix is to assign work to someone else.

EXAMPLES OF FIXES YOU CAN ALWAYS MAKE–

- Create a new contract/agreement with different terms, including how success is measured, how commitment is proven, a new set price, and bail-out/termination clauses.
- Change your role, your effort, your responsibilities.
- Get help. Get a firm commitment from someone to step in and change the situation for the better.
- Add resources. Make more money, create more available time, dedicate space.

Remember: Hope and good intentions are not action. Either Fail Fast or Fix Fast and move forward.

What to Do with Decision Failures—A Review

As a quick review, our reaction to decision failure is important to limit the damage via the three helpful approaches:

1. Control the mental chaos in our heads and recognize when we are not thinking clearly.
2. Avoid the errors of deflection, defending sunk costs, Accepting the Unacceptable, and Goal Grooming.
3. Make a solid second decision to minimize the near-term damage and the long-term impact and move forward. Either Fail Fast or Fix Fast.

PERSONAL EXERCISE: Fail or Fix?

What failure is at the top of my mind that most needs to Fail Fast or Fix Fast so I can move forward positively? For this important exercise, please make a handwritten response. Perhaps use a separate sheet of paper to record your thoughts.

Learning from Failure

The best thing we can do with failures in our decision making is understand how we put ourselves in the position to fail. Were we aware of the needed details? Did we make bad assumptions? Do we repeat the same mistakes? Was I The Decisionator when I made that decision? We cannot be a perfect judge of people or ideas or any other decision category. Thus, failures are best reviewed and memorized for *why* the failure occurred—which demands that we take responsibility for the original decision. We accumulate wisdom as we learn familiar patterns with ourselves, other people, etc. If we can perform an autopsy on a bad decision and conclude why and how we failed, we will spot the pattern and be in a position to recognize the same damaging path next time—sharpening our decision-making discipline. Over time, you will know your tendencies, such as—

"I make the worst decisions when I am stressed."

"I cannot make great people decisions. I am blinded by hope."

"I should never buy expensive items by myself."

"I tend to overcommit because I cannot tell others no."

"I hurry my decisions because I want to get going and I must slow down."

"My decisions usually include justifying the decision with good intentions that I fail to deliver."

"I tend to give other people too much credit in my decisions and I am usually disappointed."

"My search for the ideal romantic relationship has grown to dominate my thinking."

PERSONAL EXERCISE: A Big Fail

What was the root cause of my last big decision failure? For this important exercise, please make a handwritten response. Perhaps use a separate sheet of paper to record your thoughts.

- What did I learn about myself from it?

·12·

CLEANING UP THE PAST AND PRESENT

"My point is, life is about balance. The good and the bad. The highs and the lows. The piña and the colada."

—ELLEN DEGENERES

What can your life look like when you put all of this insight into practice? You now have a big advantage you can use. All of our work thus far in this book serves to emphasize the importance of decisions in our life outcomes, our often-flawed role as the decision maker, and how to recognize bad decisions.

Instead of simply accepting what happens and living with reduced life goals, we have the ability to adjust our decision making to create new dividends and be happier.

You are walking the earth more prepared than ever before. Let's get started.

Your Whole Story

Let's fast-forward with mental imagery to get you thinking about your future. Regardless of your current age, at the end of your life, you will have collected a lot of memories and you will have accomplished a lot. Imagine you are reviewing your life's highlight film, watching your favorite moments, your travels, your life milestones, your contributions, and your relationships. Is that the *whole* list of highlights you always wanted? Or are they just *some* of what you wanted?

The decisions you make from this point forward will either *add* or *delete* significant points in your life's highlight film.

So what is your whole story going to be? You are the driver, and your decisions are the highway on-ramps and off-ramps. The tools in this book combined with your fierce determination will get you what you desire for your life's highlight film. It won't be a matter of if. It will only be a matter of *when*.

Undoing Past Decisions: STOP and REVERSE

Now that we are determined and we are envisioning what we want in the end, we need to work on our past and present. We cannot make things change just because we think. We have to act. Yet you may have limited flexibility—you may have ropes that bind you from past decisions—that prevent you from moving forward the way you want. Think back to your Regret Inventory and consider your present freedom . . . are there any past decisions you should stop and reverse?

To help you consider this important subject, the following questions can help you. It may help you to pretend you are someone else looking at your life and being brutally honest.

"Starting over can be the scariest thing in the entire world, whether it's leaving a lover, a school, a team, a friend or anything else that feels like a core part of our identity but when your gut is telling you that something here isn't right or feels unsafe, I really want you to listen and trust in that voice."

—JENNIFER ELISABETH,
BORN READY: UNLEASH YOUR INNER DREAM GIRL

PERSONAL EXERCISE: What to STOP

For this important exercise, please make a handwritten response. Perhaps use a separate sheet of paper to record your thoughts.

1. For me to achieve the success I want, I need to stop these relationships:
2. For me to achieve the success I want, I need to get rid of these things that cost me too much money to keep:

Continued

3. For me to achieve the success I want, I need to connect less with these people:
4. For me to achieve the success I want, I need to stop these commitments/obligations:
5. For me to achieve the success I want, I need to stop these meaningless activities:
6. For me to achieve the success I want, I need to stop doing these things to my health/body:
7. For me to achieve the success I want, I need to stay away from these places:
8. For me to achieve the success I want, I need to stop thinking about these things:
9. For me to achieve the success I want, I need to no longer worry about these things:
10. From all my answers above, if I were to instantly accomplish one, it would make the greatest impact upon my life to accomplish this:

PERSONAL EXERCISE:
What to REVERSE

For this important exercise, please make a handwritten response. Perhaps use a separate sheet of paper to record your thoughts.

1. For me to achieve the success I want, I need to start these relationships:
2. For me to achieve the success I want, I need to spend some money in these areas:
3. For me to achieve the success I want, I need to connect more with these people (even if currently unknown):
4. For me to achieve the success I want, I need to start these commitments/obligations:
5. For me to achieve the success I want, I need to add this activity to my daily routine:
6. For me to achieve the success I want, I need to start doing these things for my health/body:
7. For me to achieve the success I want, I need to be in these places:
8. For me to achieve the success I want, I need to start focusing more on these:
9. For me to achieve the success I want, I need to measure progress toward these things:
10. From all my answers above, if I were to instantly accomplish one, it would make the greatest impact upon my life to accomplish this:

She Said/He Said

Some of the most popular answers to the above STOPPING exercise include—

SHE SAID:

- Stop relationships with men that need "fixing."
- Stop talking to men who have no ambition.
- Stop using Facebook.
- Stop eating fast food.
- Stop one-sided friendships.
- Stop feeling guilty.
- Stop judging the mirror.
- Stop spending all my income.

HE SAID:

- Stop wasting money on women I don't care about.
- Stop being told what to do.
- Stop using dating sites.
- Stop eating an unhealthy diet.
- Stop working at a job I hate.
- Stop comparing myself to others.
- Stop spending all my income.

By comparison, the answers for what to REVERSE are much more varied because everyone has a different idea of what it takes to reverse a situation. But, interestingly, what to STOP seems common.

How to Handle STOP and REVERSE

Making changes in our lives can be a sensitive matter. We may be breaking up with someone. We may stop smoking. We may be selling a car that is too expensive and buying one we don't love. We may be ditching our friends and going to evening college classes instead of hanging out. We may be walking for forty-five minutes every evening instead of watching TV. Change is hard, but we are determined, yes? Very quickly, you can see the path to *start* a recovery from past decisions so you are in a good position to maximize the next decision you encounter.

SOME ADVICE:

- Go slow.
- Think carefully.
- Prioritize the items you want to change, #1, #2, #3, etc.
- For each item you want to change, make a plan and practice how you explain it to yourself and others. Plan for the impact of the change so your life is not in more chaos.
- Not everyone will understand. It's your life and you are #1 priority.
- Your true friends will support your decisions.
- Consider how you will measure the difference each change brings.

What If I Don't Know?

Some of these decisions are so difficult that we cannot know for sure if we should STOP something and REVERSE it. Probably one of the most difficult questions is our romantic relationship. Is it better to be lonely and no longer wasting time with someone who is never taking us anywhere we want to go? Is Mr. Right actually "Mr. Good Enough (for right now)"? Perhaps it's time to be honest. Another example is getting away from where we are and giving a new city and new friends a chance to improve our lives. I've met so many people who have regretted that they never went anywhere because it was easier to stay in one place. ***Perhaps you don't take enough chances on people and things that could make a significant positive impact.***

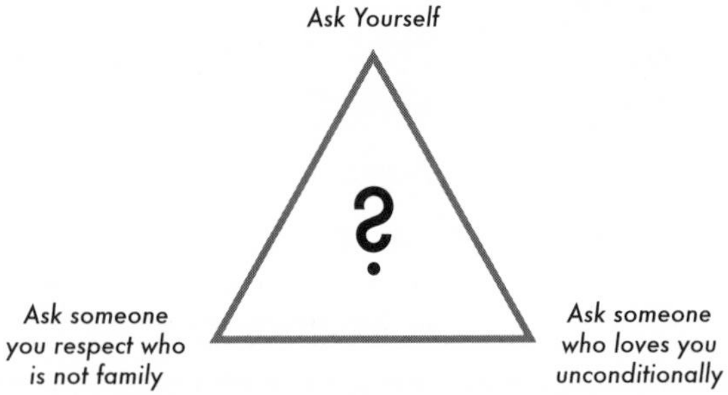

Decision Triangulation

For any of these tough decisions, after you have thought about it, do one more thing: Ask someone else their opinion. Form a perspective triangle by including three people in the answer: you, someone who loves you unconditionally (like family), and someone you respect who is not family. Add up all three perspectives and you, like a GPS signal, will pinpoint a good answer.

Summarizing Your Determination and Cleanup Efforts

As a big part of your new future, your commitment today is to enact positive change. You are determined to affect your destiny. Part of that commitment involves cleaning up decision baggage you have collected thus far, "cutting the ropes that bind you." Change is difficult. However, you have a good list of what you should STOP and what you should REVERSE. If you work these lists, I guarantee your life will be more likely to bring you new joy as you see progress toward your dreams.

·13·

MOVING (AND LIVING) FORWARD

My family and I took our seats around the large table and cooking area. It's our favorite Japanese steak house where they cook teppan style and the chef works over a hot grill with multiple clanging spatulas. It's fast and furious . . . and delicious. I ordered my usual Sapporo beer and settled in.

My family occupied five of the seats, and another family filled the remaining five. I watched the chef with interest, as I fancy myself a decent cook. He readied his tools and the many ingredient containers. From left to right he wrote down our dinner orders. As he wrote down my order for "steak and shrimp," I suddenly likened this to writing down a goal. As he went around the table, he had written and collected ten goals. I reasoned that if he did well with all ten goals, he should achieve a large tip. That seemed fair.

We proceeded through the appetizers and I watched the chef quickly cook the entrees we eagerly awaited. I noticed that he always cleaned his utensils, he was careful to keep ingredients separate, and he always had the cooktop temperature matching the food he was cooking. But most of all, he never burned the food. In all the chaos of cooking fast and cooking different dishes for ten people using different meats and vegetables, the one rule that prevented disaster was to never burn the food. It made me think: If we are the chef in our lives, we should never burn our goals with a bad decision—else our goals will taste like something we didn't order.

Too Serious and Not Fun

"This decision-making discipline is making life not fun!" your subconscious mind may shout at you. This is a perfectly natural feeling, as we humans don't want to think so hard all the time and we like to have carefree fun. I have thought about this problem by asking the question: How can successful decision makers have fun and be spontaneous while also paying close attention to the bigger moments? My answer came to me as I pondered a lady's purple-highlighted hair sitting next to me on the airplane. We don't have to be so serious about everything.

Remember this diagram?

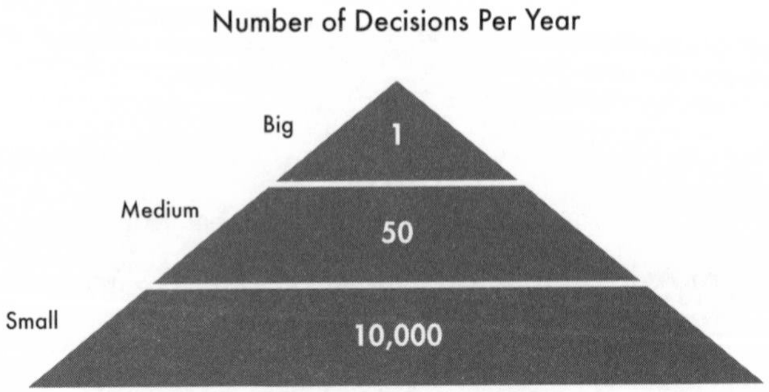

Chapter 3 discusses the *size* of decisions, and this diagram shows the approximate frequency. Big decisions have the greatest impact on our lives, medium decisions greatly affect the course adjustments of our lives, and small decisions require a lot of time/energy, but each does not carry significant weight.

We can have fun with decisions by exercising more carefree and creative and spontaneous behavior with the *small* decisions we make every day. There are so many opportunities! The clothes we wear, what we cook/eat, who we call, where we have coffee, what movie we see Friday night . . . have fun with these. There is no long-term horrible result when we play with small decisions, and we can look at decisions as a fun experiment. If you want purple hair, do it for fun (just not before a job interview). I've learned to do this with parenting. With my first child, every decision seemed big. With my middle child, I've learned to not sweat the small stuff. When my daughter wanted to double-pierce her ears, I thought about the decision sizes, small, medium, and big. Second-pierced ears are a small decision because she had already pierced her ears once as a teenager (a medium decision at the time). A tattoo, at any time in life, would be medium! What classes she takes in her junior and senior years in high school are medium because they determine college entrance eligibility. To what universities she applies is a big decision. What she wears or what movie she sees or what color she adds to her hair on the weekend are small decisions, and I don't spend my parent capital debating the small decisions. I suppose I will need to stick to this discipline when she brings a boy home . . . I hope I'm ready.

Come Back to This Book

The greatest gift you can give yourself along the way is reassurance that you are approaching your life in the best way possible to get what you want from it. Reassurance makes us feel better, and it acts like a compliment and validation rolled together. Reread some key points in this book on occasion—and review your recent life perspective and decisions you've made. If you are drifting away from some of the discipline, come back to it. If your Prime Goals need a review or you need to review the things you wanted to STOP and REVERSE, come back to this book.

Yes, each of us will mess up somewhere along the way. We can count on it. However, other people may play a bigger role in derailing our progress. Recognize that you can only drive your car and you cannot control all the other drivers on the road. Just like we commute to work or school, we have the destination in mind. Regardless of what other people (crazy drivers on the road) may do, we must be resilient and remain focused upon the destination we desired all along.

A New Approach for Regret

Along our resilient road we will certainly be bruised by bad decisions that turn to regret with confirmation that we chose poorly. The healthier approach for you to take is to swiftly dispose of regret as it happens. You can do this because you know why it happened and how to prevent it going forward.

"OK, so I have regret because of this past decision:"

"The choice that I made (at the time) was incorrect because:"

"I forgive myself. It's water under the bridge. I cannot change it now."

"I will not carry this regret as baggage.
I have learned from it and am moving forward."

Reviewing the Success Formula Waterfall

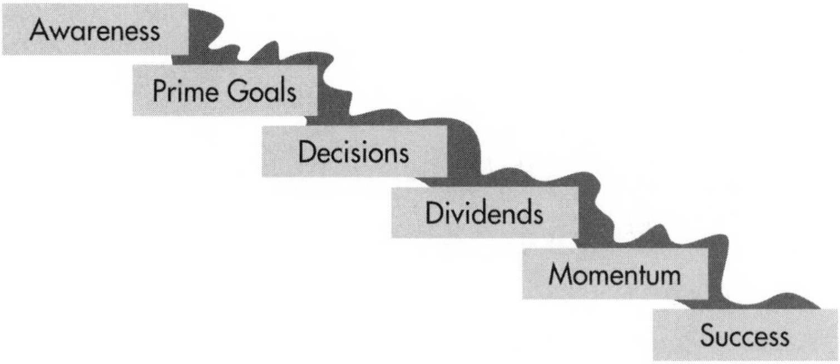

Success is at the end of the waterfall. Let's start at the top and review. Each fundamental we have covered in this book is a stage in this waterfall, cascading downward to pour success over our heads in the way we want it.

Awareness: Maintaining an awareness of all decisions is a great start. Carefully handling the Biggie Decisions affects our life more than anything we can do. We need to be aware of the exponential power of these decision categories:

- Education
- Whom to Take as Life Partner and When
- Having Children and When
- Our Social Circle
- Where to Travel/Live
- Mentors and Career Choice
- Debt and Leverage
- Health and Lifestyle
- Hobbies/Activities
- Lifetime Curiosity
- Business Partner(s)

We make about one big decision each year, so the opportunities are few to impact your life positively or negatively. We get out of practice on these, so we must be ready.

Prime Goals: We learn to set goals and distinguish which goals are Prime Goals. Then we focus upon our top goals in our decision-making process. We always keep in mind what we will not accept.

Decisions: Our Prime Decisions are the decisions that overlap our Prime Goals. They impact the Biggies in our life, and we must be aware of them and take the time and be in the right mindset to make a good decision.

Dividends: The power to get what we fully want out of life comes from Decision Dividends (Free Time, Good Health, Money,

Freedom, and Momentum) from Prime Decisions. These feel fantastic, like having your toes in the sand, the sun on your face, and a piña colada in your hand. Negative dividends create pain: anxiety, regret, and consequences . . . bringing storm clouds and sharks to your beachfront experience.

Momentum: A Decision Streak speeds up the attainment of our goals because we enjoy momentum when on a streak. Momentum helps us pick up speed and waste less time and effort.

Success: This is what you wanted. It's different for every important area of your life. Did you want to be married? Live in a big city? Travel the world? Study abroad? Start a business? Have a family and/or two golden retrievers? Success is yours to define.

If we do these things in the right order, success happens naturally. When we ignore one of them, things get off track. For instance, ***failing to define your Prime Goals will lead to drifting into outcomes you don't want.*** Take a mental picture of the Success Waterfall and it will help you imagine the lifelong process you can follow.

This Is You Now

At a fork in the road, you choose wisely. You have abandoned the common decision-making process of trial and error. That unreliable method has been replaced by a more precise personal toolkit. You are much more comfortable in your life plan for two primary reasons: (1) You now understand the differences and merits of different types of decisions—and are focused mostly on only the most impactful; and (2) with that focus and by achieving better outcomes on the most impactful decisions, you accelerate your pleasant results in life.

Your relationships are better formed and understood, your income sources are stronger, and your achievements will come into focus with newfound efficiency. You are not anxious when decisions present themselves. You walk confidently toward your goals and polish your skill of choosing well among all options. Your results include things you can measure: time saved, less stress, more joy, more momentum, more goals attained, more income earned, greater self-awareness, and a sense of power over your future. You go forward in the world more boldly, hesitate less, take on more, choose more selectively, and are rewarded more often.

This is the confident "new you." Your decision to read this book will create incredible dividends for you going forward. If possible, share what you have learned with a good friend.

Write the Next Chapter

This is an exciting time for you. Tomorrow there *may* be a decision you will make differently. Next week there will *probably* be a decision you will make differently. Next month, there will *certainly* be a decision you will make differently. You are ready. By reading this book you are carrying more knowledge about decisions than ninety-nine percent of the population, and you can use it to create the life you want.

It's challenging and empowering to think about your life as a collection of decisions you will make to affect how it turns out. Thinking about life in phases, or chapters, is a great perspective. In that mode, we can ask ourselves, "How do I want this chapter to go?" Like any good writer, we develop each chapter with the end of the book in mind.

It is time for me to turn this story over to you. You are now the author of your story from this day forward. I am incredibly excited for you. You can make a fresh start today. I have written every word of this book thinking about you—culminating in how you feel at this moment. I know you can take what we have learned here and help yourself as well as others. I wish for you the very best in life. Please remember that success for you is a personal concept. It is whatever you want it to be, and you do not have to copy other people. Be happy for yourself first, and everyone around you will be happier, too. Trust yourself and your new decision-making tools to create momentum toward what you want. You have performed your own Decision Makeover. Oh, and when you notice a decision is approaching, smile and tell yourself, "I've got this!"

ACKNOWLEDGMENTS

Taking inventory of the people in my life for whom I am grateful is my most powerful centering exercise. My gratitude to these people leaps beyond these pages with a spirit and energy that is forever.

First, I am thrilled to thank my lovely and talented wife, Amy, who has been my best decision in so many ways. I aspire that this feeling is mutual! Through twenty-five years of entrepreneurial ups and downs, crazy ideas, and ten projects always in progress with zero completed, she has weathered it all with a smile and understanding. I am certain that our ability to raise our kids well while balancing my work responsibilities is due to her untiring ability to organize, systematize, and pack full our blessed life. Amy is proof that a supportive partner enables any writer, artist, or entrepreneur to freely create and reach higher. I endeavor to do the same for her.

My children have earned acknowledgment here for a variety of reasons, most certainly because they have been great source material for this book. While I could remember many youth choices I faced, my children modernized this view. Kids, you have made good decisions so far. Trust your instincts, as they are very good. As you know, your dad is a free spirit and always ready with the "fix" to anything. Thank you for not rolling your eyes as much as you could have! You are each a very beautiful person inside and I thank you for showing me how to understand patience, humility, uncertainty, and unconditional love. I am most proud when I hear you ask great questions about the world and life situations while also exhibiting a warm heart toward others.

I find a different reason every year to be thankful for my parents as I peel the onion of wisdom and understand how their support and loyalty has always been steadfast, even if they didn't agree with me or understand my logic. I admire their quiet yet significant lifetime achievements. Mom and Dad, to your credit, you have successfully implanted in my brother and me the work ethic to aim high and make it happen. In retirement, I love that you continue to challenge yourselves to learn and do new things.

To my younger brother, I wish to tell you that I admire you. Our parents could not have had more divergent children and that difference has been valuable to me. I am your fan and I see no limits to what you can do. Your support and great questions are uniquely valuable to me.

The team at Idea Gateway is fantastic in its support of my endeavors. We turn ideas into businesses—which is very difficult—like a baseball hitter swinging hard but also attempting to never strike out. It is risky, artful, and beautiful when the genesis reveals fruit from our labor. The creative spirit is intoxicating, and I appreciate this group very much.

Mentors have played a huge role in my life, and I tell my children a mentor is one of the most rewarding relationships we can have in life's journey. I wish to earnestly thank: William (Bill) Weitzel, PhD, who taught me to look at organizations and coalitions in a predictably human way when desiring changes; Richard (Dick) Theriault, who was my early career coach (a la Bill Parcells style)—with a knowing smile and tough love, he demonstrates for me a life well-lived; and Robert (Bob) Williams, CPA, my first finance professor, CPA and advisor who recognized early that I like to chase multiple rabbits at the same time, and he encouraged me to just catch *one*.

The research for this book focused upon interviews of various people to understand decisions and circumstances at different stages of life. Notable collectors and contributors I wish to thank include: Tracie Laymon (Hollywood writer/director), Dennis Zedrick (master entrepreneur), Nicci Atchley (social media super influencer) and her father, Dr. Monty Atchley, Kellye Kamp (mid-life restart expert), Tracy Terry (super mom and single parent), and anyone else I peppered with questions about decisions in their life.

I wish to thank the very talented people at Greenleaf Book Group who are an amazing resource for a first-time author. Additionally, I believe I have the best, most tenacious book editor in Chris Benguhe. Thank you, Chris, for reminding me to always clearly answer, "What is this book is about?" Greenleaf and Chris Benguhe were great decisions for me.

INDEX

C

D

E

F

G

U

V

W

Y

ABOUT THE AUTHOR

A lifelong and successful entrepreneur, Mike Whitaker is an expert on personal and professional decision-making, turnarounds, and strategic planning. He is a no-nonsense business coach as well as speaker on topics that involve critical thinking about the future, offering unique perspectives and world-class solutions to help people achieve their goals.

Whitaker is the founder of Idea Gateway, a company that specializes in launching new businesses, providing expertise and capital for entrepreneurs. He is also a founder and board member for RevTech, a Dallas-based technology accelerator, and serves as Chairman of Lucas Color Card, a data product manufacturer he founded in 1995. These endeavors put Whitaker on the front lines of what is changing in business, technology, and for the American worker.

As part of his desire to offer helpful tools for motivated people, he has launched two new platforms: *The Idea Filter*®—an online idea assessment to help entrepreneurs separate the worthy concepts from the rest—and *The Institute for Self-Reliance*—an online source for American workers who want to take control of their futures and their careers in an uncertain economy.

Whitaker received his bachelor's degree in Cognitive Psychology from the University of Kansas and earned his MBA from the Price College of Business at the University of Oklahoma. He is married and has three children who are also on the journey of discovering their passions, goals, and paths toward success. While his passions include family balance, entrepreneurship, and helping people achieve their dreams, he also participates in competitive trapshooting, the sport of his choice.